Unexpected Gifts
Solve Tough Problems with Adaptive Positive Deviance

www.PlexusInstitute.org

Published by Plexus Institute, Washington, DC, 2017

$19.99

ISBN 978-0-692-95044-9

51999>

9 780692 950449

"...the most important thing a facilitator can do is to notice and capture the butterflies. Butterflies are those lovely, often small ideas that someone will float into a conversation. These ideas are often either so very small, or so obvious, that we in regular practice frequently fail to capture them, because we don't explicitly notice them. When we don't explicitly notice these butterflies, we miss an opportunity to turn them from ideas into action. Everyone's job is to capture those butterflies."

– Daniel J Pesut, PhD, RN, Professor of Nursing at the University of Minnesota School of Nursing and Director of the Katharine J. Densford International Center for Nursing Leadership.

"The simple rules of engagement may be simply put as the normative practices toward success but, they require discipline and meaningful intentionality to unfold successful efforts. I believe that bringing the appropriate constituents into an engrossing transaction that provides them with these norms and with the information, data, and resources necessary to inform the task, are essential to promoting positive change."

–Andrew Jay Svedlow, PhD, Professor of Art History, University of Northern Colorado

"Adaptive Positive Deviance is a truly disruptive innovation. It's both inspiring and humbling: once you've experienced it, it will forever transform your thinking about process improvement, staff and customer/patient engagement, and leadership. This book will get you off to a great start with a wealth of practical tips and great questions."

–Anthony Suchman, MD, Founder and Senior Consultant at Relationship Centered Health Care, Rochester, NY

"Projects come and go, and don't solve problems -- or change dysfunctional systems. Experts are good at naming problems, then offering canned solutions, and are usually wrong about both. Leaders fail to either lead or follow effectively. Today's young generation is the first to expect the future to get worse. Overlapping crises -- climate change, growing inequality, political polarization, community violence, disempowering globalization -- are crushing human hopes. Where does that leave communities determined to forge a sustainable future? Adaptive Positive Deviance offers a transformative way forward. Spoiler alert: The unexpected gift flows from integrating transdisciplinary research on effective change processes, practice wisdom, complexity theory, systems understandings, evaluation lessons, and case exemplars. How, what, why, when, where, and who --Kipling's six servants of honest inquiry -- are all here. Want to hang onto doom and gloom? Look elsewhere. Want to be informed and inspired? Unwrap the unexpected gift."

–Michael Quinn Patton, Author of Principles-Focused Evaluation: The GUIDE

Table of Contents

Acknowledgments

This field guide is the result of many dedicated and passionate professionals committed to helping improve communities and organizations in the US and around the world. Plexus Institute is a convening organization for professionals and others from widely diverse backgrounds and experiences who are interested in how to create sustainable change for the better, using principles from complexity science. Plexus Institute is a membership organization and we welcome all life-long learners to join us for riveting conversations, deep exploration and joyful practice.

There have been too many Plexus Institute contributors to acknowledge each one individually, however, some contributions must be called out: Lisa Kimball, Henri Lipmanowicz, Keith McCandless, Jeff Cohn, MD, Margaret Toth, MD, Mark Munger, Jon Lloyd, MD, Michael Arena, Curt Lindberg, Brenda Zimmerman, Ori Brafman, and Judah Pollack have made lasting impacts on our thinking and practice and the work here is offered with our thanks to them.

Marion Zeitlin, and Jerry and Monique Sternin conceptualized and operationalized Positive Deviance as a way to make lasting improvements on intractable problems. Around the globe, hundreds of communities and thousands of practitioners are using and iterating their ideas to make concrete improvements that matter. The Plexus network of practitioners has been a significant part of using and honing these approaches in the US and abroad and we gratefully acknowledge your generous co-learning.

Photo Credit: Unknown, Plexus Institute

You can learn more about Plexus Institute at www.plexusinstitute.org.

About the Authors

Sharon Benjamin, PhD, is a prac-ademic, she helps organizations marry classic quality improvement and organizational change methodologies with emergent technologies such as Adaptive Positive Deviance (APD) and Liberating Structures, which are rooted in complexity science. She has been an adjunct in the NYU Executive MPA program for 12 years and also teaches in the Organizational Dynamics program (MSOD) at UPenn.

Denise Easton, MS, is an entrepreneur and consultant who finds inspiration at the "complex and emerging intersections" of strategic change management, human and organizational systems, and business innovation. Denise is the co-founder and principal consultant with Complexity Space Consulting and CEO of Adapt Knowledge, a knowledge management consulting and learning services firm. Denise recently authored *Complexity Works!: Influencing Pattern-Based Change in Teams and Organizations* (2016) and co-authored a course for the Plexus Institute titled The Complexity Lens.

Laura Gardner, PhD, a letterpress printer and book artist, prepares university students to be artist-teachers. She has received numerous grants and awards in the areas of pedagogy, arts education, book arts, and letterpress printing, and most recently led a National Endowment for the Humanities Summer Seminar for College Teachers in a transdisciplinary investigation into the commonplace book. Together with Elizabeth Minnich and Brenda Sorkin, she authored Present Teaching: We Are Creating the Future Now, in *Liberation to Civilization: Seizing an Alternative Education* (2016), Marcus P. Ford & Stephen Rowe, Editors.

Irene McHenry, PhD, is a licensed psychologist, organizational consultant, executive coach, program designer, curriculum developer, trainer and author, most recently of *The Autism Playbook for Teens* (2014). She is the visionary co-founder of a small elementary school, a grade 6-12 school for students with learning differences; a doctoral program in educational leadership and change; and a premiere leadership development program for administrators in independent schools. She is passionate about developing programs on innovation, leadership, and change for diverse populations.

Prucia Buscell is communications director for Plexus Institute and has written extensively about complexity science. With Arvind Singhal and Curt Lindberg she co-authored the books *Inviting Everyone: Healing Healthcare through Positive Deviance* (2010) and *Inspiring Change and Saving Lives the Positive Deviance Way* (2014). She has worked as a freelance writer and was formerly a newspaper reporter who won awards for investigative and public service journalism and women's interest writing.

David Hutchens, designer. David is a bestselling author who writes about learning in organizations. His books have been translated into more than a dozen languages. His new book is *Circle of the 9 Muses: A Storytelling Field Guide for Innovators & Meaning Makers* (Wiley, 2015). Learn more at www.DavidHutchens.com

Dedication

The team of authors wishes to dedicate this work to the mentors and colleagues who profoundly and lastingly shaped our lives and work. These individuals saw something in us that they supported, helping us hone our gifts with information, introductions, inspiration, curiosity and encouragement.

- Michael Arena and Bill Kirkwood, fellow travellers and scholars, who helped me understand that there's no such thing as "organizational change" only aggregated individual change, and then supported my change within to effect change without. (Sharon Benjamin)

- Lisa Kimball, mentor, friend and master translator of the complex into the human. Her genius is to recognize and nurture the butterfly's emergence by releasing it only when it is ready to make a difference. Larry Solow, a business partner whose generosity and belief in the "co" of everything makes all our work the best we can bring. (Denise Easton)

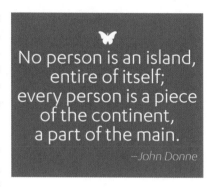

No person is an island, entire of itself; every person is a piece of the continent, a part of the main.
–John Donne

- Lilian Moore, poet, editor, teacher. Through hours of conversation, and by her own model, Lilian showed me that a successful professional woman in the arts brings others along with her. (Laura Gardner)

- Polly Young-Eisendrath, psychologist, writer, Jungian analyst, mindfulness teacher, Vermont. Polly put me on a path of insight and learning that led to my becoming a psychologist. I have great gratitude for her deep listening, skilled teaching, and profound understanding of love. (Irene McHenry)

- Si Liberman, the humane and imaginative former Sunday Editor of The Asbury Park Press, in New Jersey, urged his staff to be alert for stories and the stories behind the stories: his instruction was find the people, learn the issues, get it right and get it written. Curt Lindberg, founder of Plexus Institute, hired me and provided the opportunity to learn about the endlessly fascinating field of complexity science. I am grateful to both. (Prucia Buscell)

We hope reading this book helps you think about new ways to tackle a tough problem, and that these ideas and techniques light your path.

Introduction to
Adaptive Positive Deviance (APD)

The First Story: Shrimp, Crabs and Greens

When Positive Deviance pioneers Jerry and Monique Sternin went to Vietnam in 1990 for the US NGO Save the Children, nearly two thirds of children in the country were malnourished. Their mission was to improve childhood nutrition throughout the country, and the Vietnamese government gave them six months to show success with "a lasting impact."

They had to find a way to get results faster than would be possible with any conventional nutrition effort. They knew Tufts University nutrition professor Marion Zeitlin had used the concept of Positive Deviance years earlier when she studied why some very poor children were healthier than peers in equally poor households. So, the Sternins began what would become the first field tested PD nutrition effort.

They started in four impoverished villages. Health volunteers with bicycles and a mere six scales weighed 2,000 children under the age of three. They made a card with the name, family and weight of each child. Some 64 percent of the youngsters were seriously underweight. But some of these very poor families had children who were well nourished and healthy. The Sternins and their Vietnamese helpers visited the families of the well nourished children and carefully observed how they gathered, cooked and ate their food. The families of well nourished children had the exact same resources as their equally impoverished neighbors. But their practices differed.

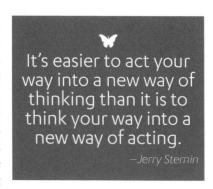

It's easier to act your way into a new way of thinking than it is to think your way into a new way of acting.

—Jerry Sternin

Very poor parents of healthy kids collected tiny shrimp and crabs from the paddy fields and served these with their rice. They also picked the leaves of sweet potato plants. These foods were available to everyone, but most people were unaware of their nutritional value and considered them inappropriate for eating. While it was customary to feed children twice a day, parents of the healthier kids fed them three or four times a day. They also washed their children's hands before and after meals, reducing the likelihood of infectious illnesses and intestinal problems.

The Sternins knew that just telling others what to do wouldn't work, because new ideas are often rejected. Educational classes might also be ineffective because knowledge does not always lead to action. Community members in each of the four villages worked with the Sternins to design nutrition programs that would let families see why and how some kids were flourishing. Mothers of healthy and malnourished children helped each other forage for shrimp, crab and greens. Mothers of malnourished kids learned from experienced mothers how to cook the new foods. As their children ate together, all parents saw that the children ate more and wasted less when they had smaller meals more often. The practice of hand washing also spread. Parents who saw their own kids getting healthier readily adopted the new practices. After a two year pilot project, malnutrition in the four communities had declined by 85 percent. In later studies Emory University researchers found successive generations of children in the impoverished villages were all well nourished. After several years, the PD nutrition intervention became standard practice nation-wide in Vietnam.

The keys to adoption of new practices, the Sternin believed, are doing, not telling, and action that leads to knowledge. As Jerry Sternin always emphasized, "It's easier to act your way into a new way of thinking than to think your way into a new way of acting."

The Sternins developed Marion Zeitlin's research and their own experience to craft Positive Deviance initiatives they used in Vietnam and other underdeveloped countries to reduce malnutrition, human trafficking, and female genital cutting and improve infant and maternal health and school attendance. In every community, among people who had the same limited resources and faced the same obstacles, there were always some people whose practices led to better outcomes. Those existing Positive Deviant practices, once identified, could spread because they didn't require new resources, special expertise, or outside help.

Successful PD initiatives have worked in the US and other developed countries to improve health, foster better business and organizational operations, and create better conditions in prisons, the military and other institutions. Plexus Institute spearheaded a successful initiative to reduce healthcare associated infections in 40 hospitals in the US and other countries. While on this journey working with healthcare organizations, schools, community groups and prisons, Plexus and other PD practitioners noticed that the process was adapting to local conditions and needs and that the practice of PD itself was also adapting through the use of innovative approaches such as Liberating Structures (see www.LiberatingStructures.com). In some cases, where a solution to a problem did not already exist, people in the community using PD processes were able to tap the resources they had to devise a new solution of their own.

As a result of these continued creative changes, Plexus began referring to this new, larger set of practices as Adaptive Positive Deviance (APD).

To be hopeful in bad times is not just foolishly romantic. It is based on the fact that human history is a history not only of cruelty, but also of compassion, sacrifice, courage, kindness. What we choose to emphasize in this complex history will determine our lives. If we see only the worst, it destroys our capacity to do something. If we remember those times and places — and there are so many — where people have behaved magnificently, this gives us the energy to act, and at least the possibility of sending this spinning top of a world in a different direction. And if we do act, in however small a way, we don't have to wait for some grand utopian future

–Howard Zinn

What is Adaptive Positive Deviance (APD)?

Every community has examples of individuals or small groups whose uncommon and unique practices result in different and better outcomes than their peers, despite facing the same barriers and having access to the same resources. What is their secret?

There is no single answer to that question because every community or organization is unique. However, we will share how Adaptive Positive Deviance (APD) can help any community find new ways to permanently solve intractable problems by identifying solutions from within the community and its available resources.

APD is different from other practices because it recognizes that all communities, at their core, operate as a complex system of independent but interrelated humans who are continually striving to find their appropriate place and role within the communities where they live and work. Equally important is the belief that transformation begins with the stories, knowledge, and experience that already exist in the community.

> Using the great goodness of many, and actively developing the critical thinking and relational skills that make us human, we intend to astonish the world with what becomes possible when we nourish and sustain the human spirit.
>
> *—Margaret Wheatley*

The best answers emerge from within the process and the community.

This book is offered as a guide for understanding, learning, and practicing the APD process. Building on new language and distinctions found in Complexity Science, APD offers tools and lenses designed to understand, talk about, and influence change.

In every situation where APD is applied, the following insights can help guide your practice. You will become familiar with how they influence your decisions and actions.

Look for practices that might be "hidden in plain sight."

Discover the expertise already within the community.

Powerful questions set the conditions for change.

Answers emerge from within the process.

Conversations iterate throughout every APD process.

Data guides the process and metrics shape the next step.

Iteration is the practice that moves small changes toward big change.

Although there is no one right place to begin, change often begins when you see things differently, develop an inquiry-based mindset and take actions that are **iterative** and continually changing in response to circumstances and needs. An example of this is sailing a boat in stormy conditions. Even the most skilled and confident sailors need to continually shift their plan of action in response to the sudden shifts in the weather.

Adaptive Positive Deviance (APD) is a process focused on discovering and proactively developing unique, positive, and often subtle *differences* throughout a community that can generate new options and solutions. Looking to the community, not to outside experts, for data, engagements, insights, and solutions, APD emphasizes collaboration and community wide practice. The emerging options for dealing with challenges are developed and understood through a shared community context.

Adaptive Positive Deviance has been successfully used to improve patient safety in hospitals, improve the quality of life for the elderly in nursing homes, and improve teenagers' lives by reducing gang violence. APD has become a valuable tool that can improve education by enhancing teacher effectiveness amidst challenging conditions. We have found no limit to the types of communities or organizations that could find value in this action-based practice; we hope APD will add value to your community.

We invite you to begin to Look for practices that might be "hidden in plain sight" in your community.

Looking for what's hidden in plain sight. Photo Credit: Jerry Sternin

Blinded by the Obvious

The "Donkey Story," a Persian folktale, is a reminder that the answers you seek are so obvious that you often can't see what is right in front of you.

Once upon a time, there was a man called Nasrudin. He was a well-known and very successful smuggler. Every day he would bring his donkey train to the border crossing and everyday the border guards would diligently search trying to find what he was smuggling. The border guards would take every piece of straw out of the baskets. But they never found anything. Finally, Nasrudin retired as a very wealthy man. Eventually, the head of the border guards retired, as well. One day they met upon the village path, and the border guard said to Nasrudin, "Nasrudin, please, now that you are old and wealthy and retired, and now that I'm old and retired and can no longer harm you, will you tell me what it was that you were smuggling all those years?" Nasrudin smiled and said................. "donkeys!"

APD Begins with Complexity Science

This section offers insight into the importance and influence of Complexity Science on "how and why"APD works in communities. APD is a rigorous process that requires a unique set of tools for addressing and solving complex problems. A little history will help explain the difference between APD and more traditional, familiar practices, which are based on Newtonian or mechanistic approaches, in understanding and working with communities or organizations.

During the 18th, 19th and well into the 20th centuries, management theory and practice emphasized the view of humans as parts of a machine that worked together in a deterministic fashion to produce consistent and predictable results. Bureaucratic hierarchies, centralized control, discipline, division of labor, organizational charts, standardized tools and procedures, emphasis on planning rather than improvisation, and minimal relationships to those outside of the organization remain as embedded models of successful control, influence and behavior (Morgan, 1997; Plsek, Lindberg and Zimmerman, 1997).

Viewing organizations as machines assumes that problems and solutions can be explained by the careful examination of the parts. However, for many aspects of community and human behavior, outcomes are not explained by simply combining individual parts into a whole. For example, how do we explain the spontaneous self-organization of community members in response to a natural disaster or crisis when it emerges without an official plan or process?

> *The essence of self-organization is that some thing or process, A, leads to another, B, which in turn leads to more of A, triggering more B, more A, and so on in an increasing spiral of feedback... Patterns form with no need for human "intelligence" or activity... scientists and engineers have found self-organization at work in literally thousands of settings—in the biological chemistry that puts stripes on a tiger's back or a butterfly's wing, in waves on the sea, in sand dunes in the desert, or in the great cyclonic wind patterns of hurricanes. The essence of self-organization is that a pattern emerges... on its own and in a way that has little or nothing to do with the detailed properties of the parts making it up (Buchanan, 2007, pp. 12 -14).*

In self-organizing, groups of people create outcomes that have impacts far greater than could have been predicted by their collective resources and skills. The process of self-organization produces outcomes that emerge from the relationships and the context, rather than just the parts or the sum of the parts. (Zimmerman, 1999).

APD practitioners recognize that all communities, at their core, operate as complex systems organized around certain broad characteristics. They

- organize around a recognizable social arrangement (an organization, school, not-for-profit group, government institution, a neighborhood);

- pursue collective goals;

- attempt to govern and control their own performance;

- construct "boundaries" that separate and identify them within their larger external environments.

Another important distinction inherent in complex systems is that individuals, groups, and the larger community itself often face similar complex challenges based on unpredictable interactions. One advantage of an APD mindset is that new perspectives emerge when we recognize that all parts of communities operate as *complex adaptive systems*, embodying the qualities of a living system that changes over time.

In a large medical center, one staff member searched until he found the simple solution he suspected would solve an apparently complex problem. Nurses were complaining they had to carry containers of hot water from other parts of the building because only cold water came from the faucets in their floor. A disruptive multi-million dollar renovation at the center had just been finished. Engineering and planning personnel confirmed the lack of hot water and contemplated an expensive plumbing project. Nurses called a maintenance staffer. He looked deep into the pipes and found a valve with settings that had been hidden by splash of paint. After his reset, hot water flowed.

How Complex Adaptive Systems Work

Complex adaptive systems consist of groupings of individual agents (ranging from teams to entire organizations or communities), who have the freedom to act and react in unpredictable ways, and whose actions are interconnected such that they produce system-wide patterns. (Easton and Solow, 2016)

Complex adaptive systems have many characteristics and properties. The attributes most helpful for working with APD are: connectivity and co-evolution, emergence, iteration, nested systems, patterns, self-organization, the part-the whole-the greater whole. These terms and definitions are included in the next section: Key Terms and Vocabulary.

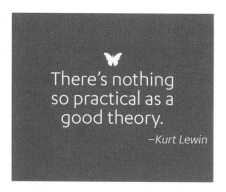

There's nothing so practical as a good theory.

–Kurt Lewin

Is Your Community More Like a Machine or a Garden?

This question is a favorite starting point for helping a community recognize why current solutions (designed with machines in mind) do not adequately address complex problems in complex environments. The machine metaphor adheres to the core principle that it is possible to find one best way to perform and manage tasks, and then predict and produce consistent outcomes. The machine metaphor continues to be a preferred management approach in large part because of its

- physicality (machines can be seen and touched);

- ability to be assembled and disassembled (machines can be fixed);

- relative ease of operation (machines can be controlled); and

- highly predictive nature (machines do what we expect).

The garden metaphor reflects very different operating conditions, with frequent changes and out-of-direct-control challenges obscuring cause and effect relationships. Combined, this makes purely rational decision-making ineffective. Even a master gardener cannot control the weather, pests that are no longer controlled by spraying, and a shortage of skilled workers due to unanticipated immigration changes.

A different set of competencies and tools are needed to succeed when the operating conditions are characterized by

- indirect linkages of cause and effect;

- levels of input/cause may not be proportional to output/effect;

- no "one best way" to achieve desired results;

- acute sensitivity to initial conditions; and

- continual evolution and self-organization.

Gardening, and its related practices, benefit from thinking about the garden as a complex adaptive system. Gardens are improved when the gardener is persistent in assessing changing conditions, and when the gardener is frequently engaged in adapting to unanticipated changes in weather, precipitation and invasive species.

An apt metaphor for complex adaptive systems, "the garden," demonstrates how systems work in reality. The dynamics within a complex adaptive system offer the greatest potential for community sustainability through organic, collaborative problem solving. Yet, in many organizations today, current practices are still aligned with "the machine" model of thinking and problem-solving.

Butterfly Effect Upends the Clockwork Universe

When Edward Lorenz, a mathematician and meteorologist at MIT, was studying the problem of predictability in nonlinear weather systems 57 years ago, he made an accidental discovery that would change the course of modern science.

He was running mathematical models of 12 weather variables such as temperature, humidity and wind speed on his computer and he wanted to re-examine some earlier work. To save time, he started his previous run in the middle, and rounded off just one variable from .506127 to .506. At first, data from the two runs matched. Then the two sets began to diverge dramatically, and eventually the second run lost any resemblance to the first.

That tiny fractional change Lorenz had expected to be inconsequential allowed him to accidentally discover the phenomenon known as "sensitive dependence on initial condition," a property later recognized as inherent in all chaotic or dynamic systems.

Lorenz had unleashed a powerful insight about how systems work. Writing in the MIT Technology Review, Peter Dizikes says Lorenz's 1961 discovery overthrew Sir Isaac Newton's notion of a predictable clockwork universe. Now scientists had to grapple with the realization that predicting the future in a dynamical system is virtually impossible because the variables can never be measured without some degree of human error. The phenomenon came to be known as the "butterfly effect" after Lorenz suggested that the flap of a butterfly's wings in Brazil could ultimately set off conditions that cause a tornado in Texas. Even a tiny change could have a disportantiate effect on a massive system like the weather.

The butterfly effect ignites the imagination, in part because the visual representation of the computer model that led to Lorenz's discovery resembles a butterfly (Dizikes, P. 2011).

Key Terms and Vocabulary

The Adaptive Positive Deviance process has many foundational concepts that undergird the logic of the process. Adaptive Positive Deviance is a deliberate and intentional approach to finding solutions, and the approach is rooted in complexity science. Important concepts and vocabulary are offered here, at the outset, to provide a quick understanding of the formative ideas that coalesce in APD. Readers are encouraged to read through this material, and then refer back to these ideas from time-to-time to reground themselves as it is easy to unconsciously drift back into more traditional problem-solving approaches.

Adaptive Space

A place or time that offers unusual flexibility and possibility for collaboration and generative conversations to take place. An adaptive space can be literal or relational, existing anywhere at anytime. It is a bottom-up, grassroots activity when people decide to try new things as they adapt approaches in their respective environments.

Appreciative Inquiry

What went well? Why? Today? Yesterday? This week? This year? Last year? This structure democratizes conversations across hierarchical levels. Anyone can respond to the question, "What went well?" and the person giving the information offers a perspective on why it went well. Others may add to the "why." This simple design promotes resilience, creativity, and well-being.

Catching Butterflies

Catching butterflies is noticing when someone suggests a small, seemingly insignificant behavior that is different from the norm and results in positive outcomes. Like catching a butterfly, a gentle approach is necessary in order for the behavior, and the butterfly, to survive and thrive. It is important for the group to pause and consider even the smallest idea or observation. Anyone in the group could catch the butterfly by mirroring someone's actual words - "I think I just heard you say . . . . What do we think about that?"

Chaotic Events

Chaotic events are situations that are radically unpredictable and uncontrollable (e.g. during a natural disaster). Spontaneity, resourcefulness, and improvisation are required, rather than standard operating procedure.

Chunking

The term was coined by Kevin Kelly, a former editor of *Wired Magazine*, to explain how complex systems emerge from collections of simple components that work well independently and become building blocks for new systems. One example is the internet, which evolved in chunks. Separate components were integrated into a larger system after they had been individually tested and refined and widely accepted. In organizations, the chunks, or building blocks, could be small teams or units that work well on their own and later combine efforts with other people and other teams to create new products and systems. The process is always bottom up rather than top down.

Communities and Ownership

Communities are human systems given form by conversations that build relatedness. The conversations that build relatedness most often occur through associational life, where citizens are unpaid and show up by choice. Rather than the belief that the future will be improved by new laws and more oversight, Peter Block (2008) suggests a new context that restores community - one of possibility, generosity, and gifts, using the all-purpose ownership question: What have I done to contribute to the very thing I complain about or want to change?

Complementary Pairs

Such contraries as light and dark, good and evil, friends and enemies, have always been present in human awareness. We usually perceive them as mutually exclusive. Neuroscientist Scott Kelso (2006) says our either/or thinking tends to obscure the dynamic relationship between pairs that actually complement each other rather than being polar opposites. Neuroscientists and social scientists remind us that potential for reconciling these pairs, and for enabling understanding between diverse fields, lies in the space between them.

Complexity

Complexity is found in systems when there are unpredictable interactions of multiple participants and components across many levels of the system. School systems are complex systems of many interconnected parts that can be viewed as their own unique complex system from an individual school within a school system to a classroom right through to the family enrolled. Complex systems face complex challenges, rooted in those same unpredictable interactions present in the system itself and require different ways to address challenges. Predetermined solutions that "should" work, in theory, are often much less impactful than expected in complex environments. Approaching an issue looking for emergence is highly valuable in complex systems.

Connectivity and Co-evolution

Connectivity and co-evolution are essential to the sustainability of a complex adaptive system. How people in a system connect and relate to each other influences collective changes in system-wide patterns that impact their environment. As the environment responds to change it influences the patterns in the system, which will once again change — this is a constant process that allows the people, systems, and environment to work together for adaptive survival.

Discovery and Action Dialogue (DAD)

DAD stands for *Discovery and Action Dialogue.* One of the most productive methods used in facilitating APD is the Discovery and Action Dialogue (DAD.) Using a DAD format for conversation, the group identifies what the ideal state is, what gets in the way of achieving that, and any successful practices that overcome the barriers that they face. Those participating decide whether any of those practices are worth trying for themselves, and then create an action plan for getting that process started. DADs are one of approximately *35 Liberating Structures* (see below).

Dialogue

In APD, dialogue is a quality of conversation, of speaking and listening to create greater understanding among those in the conversation. When dialogue is generative, we experience a creative flow of ideas and insights that go beyond anything known at the outset of the dialogue. See "Generative" below.

Diversity and Difference

Research on human organizations and other complex systems has shown differences and diversity among members of teams and groups lead to better and more creative problem solving and project success. Teamwork flourishes when the perspective of members include differences influenced by race, ethnicity, gender, age, academic training, economic status and life experience.

Dynamic Tension

Change is seldom a smooth transition from the old to the new. When there is push-back or resistance to change, a dynamic tension becomes apparent between the known current reality and actions and the unknown future reality and actions. In APD, this tension indicates an important time and space for asking lots of questions, getting all feedback and encouraging experimentation.

Emergence

Emergence refers to the unpredictable events and issues that result from the interactions between people and among elements of the system. An emergence mindset is useful for supporting APD and tackling complex challenges. Emergent events, ideas, and issues are not under the control of any one person or any one part of the system. They have new elements that could not have been predicted by knowing the individual people or behaviors in the interaction. When people in various parts of the system come together, surprising outcomes "emerge" out of nowhere or have been "hidden in plain sight."

Ethnography

A means to represent the culture of a group, graphically and/or in writing. It is the systematic study of people and cultures. Ethnography is designed to explore cultural phenomena where the researcher observes society from the point of view of the subject of the study.

Facilitator

A facilitator is a volunteer leader who helps the community work together to discover solutions to complex challenges. Facilitators invite, welcome, ask questions, and use the group's prioritized agenda keep meetings moving.

Feedback

Feedback is the reciprocal effect of one system or subsystem on another. A negative feedback loop occurs when two systems dampen each other's output. Positive feedback happens when two systems amplify each other.

Generative

Generative conversations lead to discovery of new ideas, behaviors, practices and unanticipated sources of value that could not have been predicted in advance. A generative process can nurture and guide the birth of new ways of thinking and doing.

Initial Conditions

In a complex system, the initial conditions for change begin when there is greater sensitivity to an action. See the Lorenz "butterfly effect," described above. Being deliberate about choosing things, such as room set-up and meeting design are initial conditions that can make a significant difference in how successful a meeting or conversation is.

Iteration

Iteration is the act of repeating small changes in the initial conditions or current state of the system, which can significantly influence outcomes and change behaviors. A small change is often unnoticed like the "flapping of butterfly wings" yet as the change iterates and interacts with other elements in the system during each feedback loop, it serves as the engine for emergence and self-organization, resulting in significant changes to the overall system.

Liberating Structures (LS)

Easy-to-learn, simple techniques that enhance participation in groups of any size, making it possible to truly include everyone and unleash hidden ideas and feedback. Liberating Structures can be used as a disruptive innovation when overly controlling or constraining approaches leave people feeling stuck (www.liberatingstructures.com).

Newtonian Theory

According to Newtonian physics, the whole is equal to the sum of it parts. Classical physicists thought we could understand the whole by studying the parts in greater and greater detail, and that the whole and its parts constituted a linear system. Newton's laws of motion laid the foundation for classical mechanics, which gave rise to the idea that physical and human systems were also linear, were as predictable as machines, and could always be expected to obey scientifically accepted laws. That mechanistic view prevailed well into the 20th century.

Nested Systems

This concept demonstrates that most systems (communities) are embedded within other systems that are part of even larger systems. Another way to think of nested systems is to recognize that the components of a large complex system such as a government are also complex systems,

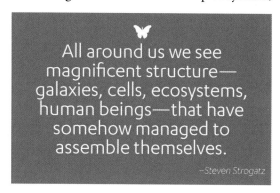

All around us we see magnificent structure— galaxies, cells, ecosystems, human beings—that have somehow managed to assemble themselves.

–Steven Strogatz

such as the judicial system, educational system, and defense systems.

Ownership

This concept focuses on individual endorsement of an idea, a decision or an action plan that you understand, believe in, have chosen to develop and are willing to implement. When everyone in the community is involved in creating the plan, there is no need for persuasive buy-in.

Paradox

A paradox is evident when two opposite points of view or understandings seem to be true. The value of a paradox, rather than trying to decide which point of view is the truth (either/or), is to explore it, study it, consider it a gift. A paradox presents an opportunity to examine long-held assumptions and discover which of them can be let go in order to have creative innovation (both/and).

Patterns

In a complex adaptive system, patterns reflect an identifiable condition or behavior that is both resilient and adaptive to the fluctuations in the system. Patterns can be influenced and change over time by the individuals, the community, the environment, and other systems.

Self-organization

Self-organization is the way in which a complex adaptive system responds to changes and makes adjustments. The system is continually adjusting to fluctuations in its environment. The process of self-organization sets the conditions for patterns of behavior to emerge from the random interactions throughout system. This process is generally spontaneous, triggered by continual and random actions. It can also be influenced by deliberate interventions. Any system of people has the capacity to be self-organizing. In organizations and communities, self organization

> The pattern . . . is there from the start. Your task in life is to discern that pattern, listen for it, and give room for it to emerge. More commonly, though, we are too busy trying to make things happen — to make ourselves happen. We may push and shove through most of a lifetime before realizing that another voice is whispering beneath the fret of our efforts and strategies. . . . A deeper, truer [self] — truer to your authentic pattern — is wanting you to follow its course. . . .
> – Roger Housden

can be jump-started using techniques, such as Liberating Structures (see above). For example: At a large meeting of several branches of an IT support division, people asked each other for help solving a difficult problem. In one group of four, a woman described the woes of her call center staff. Because they couldn't see customer records when they received a call, they had to take the customer's information, log off, log into another system, find information to resolve the issue, and then re-contact the customer. It was a time-consuming process that irritated customers and frustrated staff. Another woman in the group was surprised. "Why can't you see the customer's file? I could give you real-time access to customer data," she said. " Would that help?" These two women knew each other fairly well.

But they didn't know each other's job responsibilities. Engaged in structured work discussion, they resolved a systemic issue to improve operations of a whole staff.

Sensemaking

In APD, sensemaking is the process in which people work together to create a collective interpretation that includes multiple perspectives. This concept refers to the way in which individuals and/or groups make meaning by creating order and a collectively shared awareness and understanding of the circumstances in which they find themselves.

Simple, Complicated, Complex

Problems are seldom successfully addressed using a one-size fits all approach. In complex adaptive systems, assessing and addressing problems requires a continuum of approaches that range from simple solutions to complex change. Example:

- **Simple**: Standardized, easy replication, no expertise required to follow, such as in baking a cake. A good recipe gives ingredients and instructions. Recipes are easily replicated and following the recipe will produce nearly the same cake every time.

- **Complicated**: A formula or method is necessary with a degree of certainty; requires rigid protocols and high level of expertise, such as sending a rocket to the moon. Sending one rocket increases assurance that the next effort will be successful.

- **Complex**: Each situation is unique, so exploration is required along with curiosity and good will in the face of uncertainty, such as in raising a child. Expertise is no assurance of success. Rigid protocols have little applicability and may be counter productive. Experience helps, but raising one child is no guarantee of success with another child. Each child is unique. Results can't be replicated and the outcome is uncertain (Westley, Zimmerman, & Patton, 2006).

The Part, the Whole, and the Greater Whole

The Part, the Whole, and the Greater Whole signify that a complex adaptive system seldom exists in isolation. A neighborhood may be unique and operate within its self-defined boundaries and affiliations but it is also part of a larger community, that is part of a city, a state, a country, or a continent. The actions of any one part can be effective but when coordinated with the actions or activity of the whole, and ultimately the greater whole, the combined interactions produce a total effect that is greater than the sum of the individual elements.

Unusual Suspects

Individuals who may not be viewed as experts on the basis of title and position but who have direct knowledge or understanding of the challenge can provide an unusual influence on the project outcome. APD encourages participation by everyone because nontraditional voices add different perspective and possible solutions to existing challenges. Their unique knowledge, experience, skills, and intuition can provide unexpected contributions. When invited into the conversation, some may initially be apprehensive about whether they really have anything to contribute. Finding out how big their contribution really can be often generates tremendous energy for the project.

Wicked Questions

Wicked questions hold a special place in the art of inquiry and engagement. They embody elements of apparently irreconcilable issues that do not have an obvious or easy answer, and are used to help expose tensions and contradictions and dislodge self-fulfilling prophecies. Wicked questions open the way for new and unusual information flows while expanding possibilities for experimentation. For example, "How can identify our direction when we don't know the future?"

An Unusual Suspect Makes the "Difference that Makes a Difference"

Jasper Palmer was a patient transporter at Einstein Medical Center in Philadelphia for more than 20 years. We finish this section with Jasper's story, because it illustrates the power of actively seeking and then listening to everyone's ideas and practices.

The role of the patient transporter is to help move patients throughout the medical complex. When that patient is identified as harboring a "superbug" such as MRSA, preventing the bacteria from spreading during that transport is quite a challenge, one that even experts from the CDC hadn't figured out.

Palmer emerged as a leader in the APD project by Plexus Institute, when he pointed out that these MRSA-positive patients in isolation rooms had overflowing trash cans because hospital staff and visitors are required to put on gowns and gloves before entering their rooms and dispose of the protective gear before leaving. This created a dilemma. Upon seeing billowing trash can, does one do the right thing by wearing a gown, and add to the mess? Or, does one avoid the disposal problem, take a risk, and perform the patient task without a gown? Not only did Mr. Palmer identify the challenge, he developed a solution that worked for him and could work for others. He devised a way to quickly remove all his protective gear and stuff it into one inverted glove, compressing the voluminous possibly infected garments into a wad the size of a baseball.

Watch a video of Jasper Palmer at https://www.youtube.com/watch?v=MzxR67WnhH8

Simple Rules for Implementing APD

The idea of simple rules emerged from computer simulations of flocks of birds in flight. If the birds follow three rules—fly towards the center, avoid bumping into another bird, and match your neighbor's speed—they move together as a coherent flock. Some simple rules evolve unintentionally in small and large human societies. People in groups, communities and organizations can also deliberately develop simple rules that shape their behavior and decision-making toward collective goals. (Sull and Eisenhardt, (2015. pp. 6-7) identify four characteristics of the simple rules people use to navigate complex environments.

- Simple rules are few in number so people remember them and focus on what matters most.

- Simple rules are tailored to the group or organization using them. College athletes and middle-aged dieters could use simple rules to guide their food intake, but the rules would differ.

- Simple rules apply to well-defined activities or decisions, such as the use of triage in treating war wounds. Rules that cover multiple activities or general directives such as "do your best" are ineffective as guidelines.

- Simple rules provide clear guidance while at the same time allowing latitude for discretion. The Federal Reserve Board uses simple rules as guidelines within which they can exercise judgment when setting interest rates.

Simple Rules are not just a checklist of how to act. Complex systems are distinguished by the system wide patterns that are continually emerging. Simple rules, (intentional or not) are important to the functioning of any community or organizational system because they influence critical behavioral patterns. In APD, the use of simple rules is key to helping organizations provide a coherent way for everyone in the system to work together.

The simple rules below were refined during early APD projects to emphasize the practice and belief in inclusion, engagement, mindfulness and commitment. A brief description of each of these follows, but the value of a simple rule is how it reflects the unique spirit and actions of the community.

1. *Nothing about me without me.* When the conversation broadly includes the people most directly involved in the issue, you tap into a valuable source of positively deviant behaviors and responses to what is really happening. Why would you "Decide About Me without Me" telling you what I know and do? For example, a nurse might say: "Well, we would wear gloves if we had gloves that fit, but we often don't. A good PD response to this would be: How can we make sure gloves of all sizes are readily available?

2. *Ignore true but useless solutions (TBUs).* If a solution isn't available to all people in the community because of resource disparities, it is a true, but useless solution. If your transportation problem is solved because your rich uncle bought you a car, and none of your transportation challenged neighbors have rich uncles - that's a TBU. TBUs are noted but generally ignored in APD. The only exception would be if the resource disparity were potentially solvable and within reach of the whole community.

3. *Sitting at the feet of the staff.* Listen to the people who do the work. This can be a new, powerful way of listening and it may require a new physical posture from you as the facilitator. If you have positional authority in a group, you may choose to whiteboard a conversation — literally writing down what people with less authority are saying. You will be demonstrating that you are there to learn from the true experts — the people who actually do the work being discussed. If you are a school superintendent or principal you can have a profound impact by taking notes from a school aid or janitor in the same way that people will notice a surgeon taking notes about what

a food service worker or receptionist is saying. In APD, the staff who do the work are the first experts and most valuable resource.

4. *Take 20 seconds.* What would happen if the practice of pausing for both your own reflection and the reflection of others were part of facilitating conversations? When you take 20 seconds, you are leaving space for others to reflect and respond. 20 seconds of silence in a group can feel like a very long time – on average, facilitators begin speaking after just six seconds. The most important thing to remember here is not to begin speaking too soon after you've asked a question. Pose the question and then wait. A good way to encourage the group to respond is to look down at your shoes. This disrupts your eye contact with members of the group, signals that this is time for reflection and thinking and takes a little of the pressure to begin talking off you.

5. *Do we really have to finish what you start?* There's probably a voice in your head repeating a lesson from your childhood: *Finish what you start*! And that's effective advice in many areas of life – but it isn't especially helpful for APD. You don't have to finish, you just have to start. It's okay if you haven't answered every question or gotten every good idea from the staff about how to improve practice. Just get started and keep going!

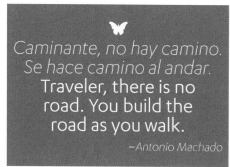

Caminante, no hay camino.
Se hace camino al andar.
Traveler, there is no road. You build the road as you walk.

–Antonio Machado

6. *Do we really want to reinvent the wheel?* Yes! In APD, reinventing the wheel often means helping staff use the basic concepts and structures developed elsewhere and adapt them for their very own unique contexts. When the community creates the wheel, they own the wheel. For example, about 40 staff members who had a monthly on-call work schedule, complained continually about evening, weekend and holiday shifts. Using APD, the group manager asked for ideas to improve scheduling. Eventually the group self organized around creating a fair on-call schedule that also met needs of their work. Complaints declined. Months later the manager marveled there were no complaints about on-call shifts for Thanksgiving. Team members had reinvented their own wheel.

7. *Sustained change grows out of owning ideas and solutions.* APD helps to create true ownership by the community and avoids the pitfalls of striving for buy-in. When it comes to solving intractable socio-technical behavioral problems, the people in the system need to own the new behaviors.

8. *Don't try to put the gold in the mine.* In APD, we are mining for nuggets of gold that already exist in the system, and APD requires trust that people in the community know best how to find them. It is our job to slow down, ask and listen, and make sense of what the people who are actually doing the work know and say about what gets in their way, who has a better way of doing something, and who else needs to be involved.

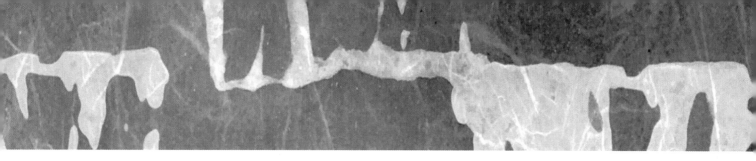

The APD Guide: Getting Started

The APD Guide: Getting Started

In the APD approach,
local innovation and collaboration
yield transformation
for the whole community

Using APD, people working together learn to transform their communities. Plexus Institute has produced this volume to assist communities and organizations seeking to improve performance in complex systems such as schools, hospitals, nonprofits, prisons and many other types of communities facing intractable problems. In addition to this book, Plexus has a companion "quick start" guidebook *Adaptive Positive Deviance: Getting Started*, 2016.

In the APD approach, local innovation and collaboration yield transformation for the whole community.

This guide is designed to support each unique community in discovering promising practices already in place, or latent, and in creating a systematic plan for sharing these practices APD is an internal, bottom-up approach rather than an externally imposed, top-down approach. Conceptually APD is an iterative methodology. Ideas are visited and revisited during the process for clarity and understanding.

The APD Guide is organized around three key phases of the APD process.

1. Pre-Launch Phase and Launch Event

2. Discover Phase

3. Confirm and Share Phases

Our Words Make a Difference

While working on nutrition improvement initiatives in the 1990s and later, Positive Deviance pioneer Monique Sternin was surprised to find many people in Cambodian villages resisted the idea of looking for successful practices among the poor. A Cambodian facilitator explained the residual fear left from a painful past. In the 1970s, the brutal dictator Pol Pot presided over the forced evacuation of the capital city of Phnom Penh and other urban areas. Pol Pot and the Khmer Rouge regime idealized the peasantry and demonized intellectuals, doctors, lawyers, and scholars. Wearing glasses could get a person killed. Professionals and students were forced to leave their homes in urban areas and join mass marches into the countryside with the expectation they would work in agriculture. Millions died along the way from torture, mass executions, forced labor, malnutrition, and disease. Decades later, a planned nutrition program was threatened by language and ideas that invoked disturbing memories. A successful program was established after the adoption of new language that allowed for culturally neutral discussion of healthy eating. (http://worldwithoutgenocide.org/genocides-and-conflicts/cambodian-genocide)

Each phase will explain the purpose and practice through easy to follow checklists and stories from the field. After introducing and launching the APD process, activities in Discover, Confirm, and Share phases are continually revisited and can happen virtually simultaneously. We have separated Discover, Confirm and Share into "phases" here for clarity and understanding.

Before we get started with our deep dive into the practice of each APD phase, the following points are foundational to developing a sound APD project initiation.

- A good APD problem

- Certain conditions must be present

- Core APD questions

- APD runs on data

- Questions that surface when getting started

Making sense of patterns with a small group of community developers. Photo credit: Sharon Benjamin

A Good APD Problem

Using APD is reserved for tough, intractable problems that have resisted solution. Not all problems are suitable for the APD process. For example, a problem that can be quickly identified, and has known available fixes, such as matching staffing needs with projected work, does not require the time and resources involved in using APD. If your challenges fall into one or more of the following categories, APD is likely to be a good fit.

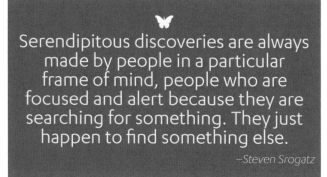

Serendipitous discoveries are always made by people in a particular frame of mind, people who are focused and alert because they are searching for something. They just happen to find something else.

--Steven Srogatz

- It is concrete, tangible, and relates to changing people's behavior.

- It is resistant to a permanent solution. You think you've fixed the problem and it shows up again sometimes in a more stubborn form. Expelling students for misbehavior usually doesn't improve school behavior.

- It is specific and measurable. For example, "improving communication" is not a good APD problem because it is too general and too hard to measure. A good APD problem might be "reducing student dropout rates from over 40% to 0."

- It is dramatic, important, and obvious, although the solutions may be subtle.

Certain Conditions Must Be Present

In much the same way careful attention to the type of problem is an important consideration, for APD to be successful, all eight of the following conditions should be present.

1. Dedicated time and space is committed to discovery, confirmation and sharing.

2. People in formal leadership roles trust that the solutions to the problem/challenge will come from within the community.

3. Leaders and community members must be willing to engage the whole system to solve the problem.

4. A compelling problem or challenge exists. The problem or challenge is visible and causes pain and hardship in the community.

5. A sense of intractability surrounds the problem or challenge. Efforts to improve have been tried with only moderate and intermittent, if any, success.

6. Data exist that reflect the severity, extent, and intractable nature of the problem/challenge. The data are readily accessible from reliable sources.

7. Evidence exists that someone somewhere in the community is getting different and better outcomes than the norm. This evidence can be both quantitative and qualitative.

8. Leadership is willing to commit the resources (people and time) to support the APD process. Conversations show that the community is realistic about the consequences of not changing and is willing to imagine a positive outcome.

The Heart of APD - Core APD Questions

Questions fuel the APD process. Asking these questions in the order presented below, and revisited over and over again, in both a linear and spiral process, keep the community on track.

- What do you *know* about the problem?

- What do you *do* about the problem?

- What gets in the way of always doing what you know you should and want to do to address the problem? What stops you from doing it every time?

- Do you notice anyone who seems to be successfully overcoming these barriers? Who? What are they doing differently?

- Who else should we be asking about this problem or that idea?

- Finally, who wants to volunteer for the next step?

If you did nothing else but ask these questions of people in your organization and acted on what you learned, you would create solutions to long-standing problems. These questions are the heart of APD, so resist the temptation to deviate from them. These questions are used as the fundamental tools of APD.

APD Runs on Data

Data can help answer key questions: How are we doing? How can we do better?

APD as a change process is informed by data. Data are collected from the beginning, in every step of the process, and openly shared with members of the community so they can examine present conditions and determine whether an intervention brings desired change. Data are a community resource. Data identify where the problems are and where solutions may be found.

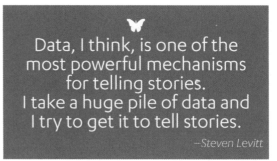

Data, I think, is one of the most powerful mechanisms for telling stories. I take a huge pile of data and I try to get it to tell stories.

–Steven Levitt

At the beginning of an APD project, it is vital to examine existing data to determine baseline information about the issue the community has decided to address. Ask, "What do the data show about the problem?" Data may suggest contradictory conclusions that will need to be examined. Can contradictions be resolved? If existing data do not seem to directly address the problem, what other data are needed and how can they be obtained? Data may come from both traditional sources such as performance reports and nontraditional sources such as student interviews. Who will be responsible for gathering additional data? How will data be reviewed and shared?

Sometimes data are not available to measure the exact things we are interested in; this is a great time to begin looking for substitutes, which are often called proxy measures. Members of the community are an important resource in identifying proxy measures. Ideas about strong proxy measures can be generated by asking people "how they know" their answers, which are often surprising and give clues about suitable proxies.

Many school systems use the number of students eligible for free or reduced price meals to gauge the portion of the school population living in poverty. In one school where teachers and administrators wanted to address violence and conflict, they began first looking closely at student absenteeism and tardiness because they believed both of those factors had underlying social, economic and emotional causes that related to student behavior and coping mechanisms in school.

Data are not just numbers and statistics. Data can be gathered from people's experiences and stories. Data can appear as patterns, such as when individual experiences and experiences that are shared by large numbers of people form recognizable patterns. For example, in parks and other public spaces foot traffic patterns are often discernible from the dirt paths worn into grassy areas. These paths tell us something about how people are navigating through the space. Very often stories that move people, stories that are personal and anecdotal, are stories that can teach. And they may hold important clues and questions about the problem. Valuable information can come from small and large group conversations, observations, repeated events and behavioral trends. It can come from letters, emails, videos and documents about the issue. Social network maps can show how information flows; they can identify people whose unrecognized expertise can be of tremendous value and identify where communication can be productively enhanced.

Statistical Surprises:
Data That Drove Life-Saving Action

In the 1850s, many people thought diseases came from supernatural causes. Medical authorities believed they came from *miasmas*—foul air arising from swamps, sewers and grime that accompanied urban poverty. In the 1854 cholera epidemic in London, physician John Snow meticulously mapped addresses of cholera victims in the Soho neighborhood and found nearly 700 people living within 250 yards of the Broad Street pump had died. That confirmed Snow's theory that cholera came from something ingested, not something inhaled. Members of the governing body didn't buy Snow's theory because the deep Broad Street well had cool clear water. But the numbers convinced them to act. They removed the pump handle, forcing people to get water elsewhere. The epidemic waned. Henry Whitehead, a young curate, set out to disprove Snow's theory. While Snow looked at the drinking habits of those who died, Whitehead studied the drinking habits of those who lived. His findings convinced him Snow was right about the Broad Street pump. Whitehead also knew people in the neighborhood, among them the family whose baby fell ill immediately before the outbreak and suffered for several days before she died. He learned the wash water from the fevered baby's soiled diapers had been dumped into a cesspool that seeped through the decaying wall of the Broad Street well, contaminating the water. Snow is considered the father of modern epidemiology. Snow and Whitehead became lifelong friends (Johnson, 2007).

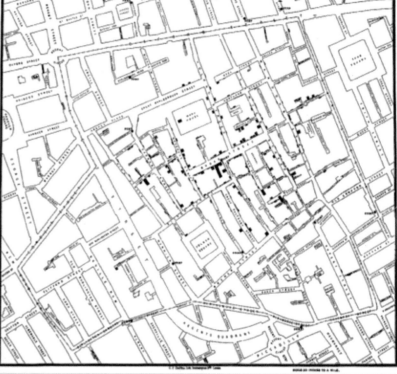

Broadwick Street showing the John Snow memorial and public house. The memorial pump was removed due to new construction in March 2016. A plaque affixed to the public house reads, "The Red Granite kerbstone mark is the site of the historic BROAD STREET PUMP associated with Dr. John Snow's discovery in 1854 that cholera is conveyed by water." Creative Commons License

Original map by John Snow showing the clusters of cholera cases (indicated by stacked rectangles) in the London epidemic of 1854. The contaminated pump is located at the intersection of Broad Street and Cambridge Street (now Lexington Street), running into Little Windmill Street.

Questions That Surface When Getting Started

These questions may have crossed your mind or come up in conversations.

How inclusive do we want to be?

APD theory assumes that we are each change agents, so we invite all community members into the creative process of change. When searching in your community for behavior and solutions that are unusually effective (positively different), it helps to broaden the conversations to include the people most involved. Bringing people together who do not normally talk with one another can be especially powerful.

Success and Storms Fueled by Small and Distant Events

Do small changes have very big effects in systems? Yes, for example, severe lightning in the Ethiopian highlands gives birth to the most devastating Atlantic hurricanes according to research from Colin Price at Tel Aviv University. Price and colleagues at Israel's Open University studied data from the World Wide Lightning Location Network and found that periods of intense lightning in eastern Africa disturb westward trade winds that travel across Africa. The resulting atmospheric turbulence creates low pressure areas known as African easterly waves, which generate tropical storms as they head west over the Atlantic (Plexus Complexity Post 5/24/07). Can you imagine? A hurricane birthed from distant lightning?

- *Why celebrate small changes big time*? After years of investing in large change efforts across our organizational systems and being disappointed in the return on that investment of time, attention and energy, APD offers a powerful new way to uncover and magnify the small changes that are worth celebrating big time. And, as you celebrate these small changes you will provide concrete evidence to participating staff that the whole system is serious about small changes and their potential for creating BIG improvements. Small successes can even enhance your local and personal climate system.

- *Do small wins fuel momentum*? Small wins fuel change by convincing people that bigger achievements are possible. B.J.Fogg, founder of the Stanford Persuasive Technology Lab, has studied "success momentum," the feeling people get when they have succeeded many times. It doesn't require a huge victory. He says our brains aren't very good at distinguishing big successes from small ones, so when people manage to change small things they get a growing sense of satisfaction and control. We can stack up lots of small wins in a short time, he suggests, and that favors more small wins and puts bigger ones in reach. As an example, he suggests tidying the house. You don't have to get the whole place gleaming. Just cleaning the bathroom sink can help create success momentum if you feel you succeeded at it (Cabane and Pollack, 2017).

How much time do we need to take in the process?

This process takes time and you will get out of it what you put into it. The APD process is not linear and may, at times, feel repetitive and slow. Stay the course and watch closely for small ideas and actions to lift up and celebrate. The APD approach is optimistic with a belief that there are solutions to the identified problem. These solutions may be hidden, so the main task is to discover them. This takes time, curiosity and patience. Progress is unlikely to be straight and linear.

Why do we celebrate small changes?

Small changes can have big effects. When using APD it is important to uncover and magnify the small changes that are worth celebrating. This creates momentum and sustains the group while improvements on larger, system-wide changes slowly come into focus and fruition. Celebrating small improvements inspires everyone to pay closer attention to small changes, which have potential for creating big improvements.

What about fun?

Yes, it is important to create fun. Creating an atmosphere that welcomes fun actually encourages creativity. When using APD, fun means establishing an informal atmosphere that is interactive, relational and full of meaningful back and forth conversation. Humor and exaggeration are important elements to light-heartedly ask about serious issues. Fun is encouraged because APD is not business as usual; it is extraordinary.

APD is about creating fun and memorable data, stories, events, and demonstrations. Much of the fun in APD is in how data are imagined, displayed, and collected. Events can include fashion shows, data potlucks, pop quizzes with give-aways like Starbucks cards, videos, Jeopardy games, balloons, bagels, unusual meeting locations, music, art materials, improvisation, building models or prototyping, and observation or "simple ethnography."

> Small opportunities are often the beginnings of great enterprises.
> —Demosthenes

> To be playful is not to be trivial or frivolous, or to act as if nothing of consequence will happen. On the contrary, when we are playful with one another, we relate as free persons, and the relationship is open to surprise; everything that happens is of consequence, for seriousness is a dread of the unpredictable outcomes of open possibility. To be serious is to press for a specified conclusion. To be playful is to allow for unlimited possibility.
> —James Carse

Chocolate Pudding: Fun and laughter boost learning

Imagine a hospital isolation room. A patient with an oozing leg wound writhes on a bed. Family and nurses stand nearby to offer comfort as a doctor bustles into the room. The doctor checks the leg, with his sleeves and necktie dangling prominently. He issues some orders, then cheerfully exchanges greetings, handshakes, and backpats with all. In a matter of moments, everything—people, clothing, bedding, and multiple surface areas are stained with brown goo.

The goo was chocolate pudding, placed to on the pretend wound to represent infectious microbes. The scene was an improv, designed by health care workers at Billings Clinic in Billings, MT, to dramatize how widely and quickly pathogens can be spread by well-intended caregivers.

The goofy vision of pudding smeared on colleagues had two immediate effects: peals of laughter and stark recognition of a serious problem.

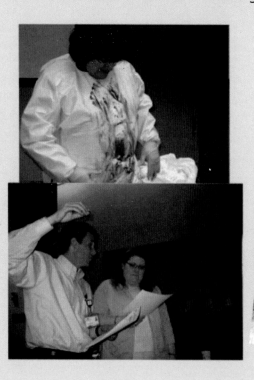

Making the invisible visible improv using chocolate pudding at Billings Clinic in Billings MT, Photo Credit: Keith McCandless

Pre-Launch Phase and Launch Event

The goal of the Pre-Launch phase is to identify the main challenge for the APD project. At its core, APD involves a commitment to the inquiry mindset. The fine art of drawing someone out by asking questions to which you don't have the answer is key to true innovation. Inquiry engages others by asking questions that are open, authentic, and honest, and to which you, the questioner, can't anticipate the answer.

Creating meaningful engagement to solve intractable problems requires both traditional(familiar) and new options and approaches. Introducing and practicing new tools throughout the APD process is an essential part of the community learning experience.

Traditional meetings are often structured like this:

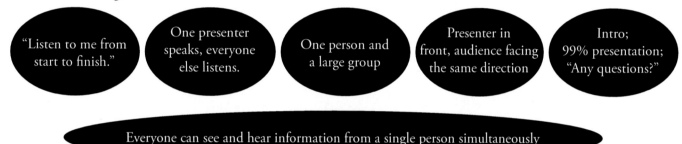

(Source: LiberatingStructures.com)

Traditional meetings rely on five primary types of interactions: presentations, managed discussion, question and answers, status reports, open discussion and brainstorming. The first three of these can be overly restrictive and the last two (open discussion and brainstorming) often open discussion up too far making it difficult to get traction.

APD meetings are often structured like this:

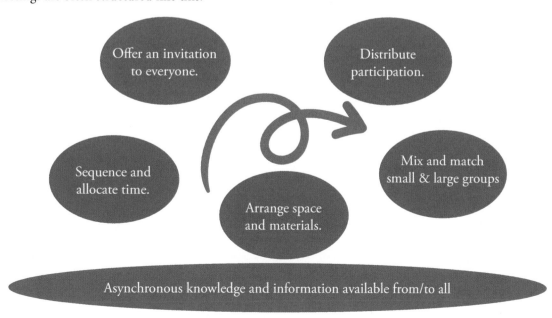

Developed by Keith McCandless, Henri Lipmanowicz, and in the early days in conjunction with Plexus Institute, Liberating Structures are powerful and engaging newer approaches that structure interactions very differently. Liberating Structures are micro-processes that help unleash the potential in groups of people to identify and grapple with difficult problems. There are currently upwards of 35 Liberating Structure techniques available at www.liberatingstructures.com.

In APD we deliberately veer toward theses kinds of newer approaches to meetings and conversation to help unleash energy and ideas in systems. In this volume we discuss two Liberating Structures at length (1,2, 4, All and Discovery and Action Dialogues) and encourage readers to explore the full menu of Liberating Structures.

Considerations Prior to Launching APD

The work done ahead of publicly launching the APD process offers a dual opportunity to quietly engage with all participants and set the expectations for everyone involved. Taking the time to more fully understand these four topics during this stage of the APD process will prove invaluable when you are ready to initiate your Launch Event.

- Review the roles

- Review the facilitator skills

- Set the expectations for participants

- Set the conditions for generative conversations

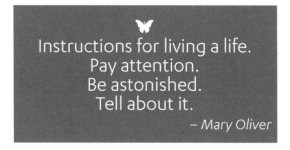

Instructions for living a life.
Pay attention.
Be astonished.
Tell about it.
– Mary Oliver

APD Roles

In APD there are roles for everyone involved, formal leaders, informal leaders, facilitators and participants. In a Complex Adaptive System, changes are continually emerging which influence everything including the roles assumed by people throughout the process.

- Formal leaders have positional authority in the system that often comes with a title such as Director, Judge, Principal, Doctor, and Counselor.

- An informal leader is someone who is passionate about the issue and who volunteers to put energy and effort into the initiative.

- An APD facilitator is a volunteer who takes on the responsibility to learn about the APD process and then facilitate the APD process in the organization.

Other volunteer informal leaders will emerge to take leadership in group meetings; these may be different people for different tasks at different times.

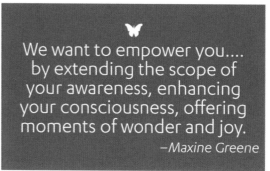

We want to empower you....
by extending the scope of
your awareness, enhancing
your consciousness, offering
moments of wonder and joy.
–Maxine Greene

The APD Facilitator

The role of an APD Facilitator is key to the successful implementation of an APD event. This checklist will help those who volunteer to serve as facilitator for engaging with the APD process and the community. It is also a valuable tool to share with the group.

An APD Facilitator should be dedicated to use and develop the following principles.

1. *Commitment to solving the problem using APD*

- Emphasizes belief that the solutions will emerge from the community

- Communicates interest in individuals and groups

- Values roles and backgrounds of all community members

2. *Interest in APD facilitation*

Notice Unexpected Subtle Differences. How Deep Was the Dip?

Positive Deviance pioneer Jerry Sternin described working on a child nutrition project in an impoverished region of Bolivia. Everyone ate the same food—a broth made from potatoes, carrots, green vegetables and bits of meat. Most children were seriously underweight. Yet some young children were better nourished than others.

Sternin and colleagues were puzzled. After many observations they discovered a small and surprising difference in food habits. Most families thought the nutrition was concentrated in the broth and they made sure their children got plenty of broth. It turned out parents of the healthier children were dipping the scoop deeper into the pot and serving their kids more of the solids.

- Experienced with small group facilitation and making space for all voices (or eager to learn with peer review)

- Intrigued by new approaches

- Believes that diverse perspectives and roles enrich the possibilities for solutions

3. *Comfort with uncertainty and open to surprises – a beginner's mind*

- Willing and able to remain curious at the edge of the known and unknown

- Willing and able to change course as new information emerges

4. *Active listening skills*

- Able to paraphrase and summarize so others know they have been heard

- Nonjudgmental approach to various ideas and input

5. *Continuous curiosity and optimism*

- Willing to ask difficult questions and willingness to set aside being the expert

- Able to recognize small, subtle differences in behavior and changes in circumstances that may be more important than they seem

6. *Believes that there are solutions to the problems identified*

- These solutions may be hidden, so curiosity and patience are key to understanding the implications of what the community is learning in the process, even though progress is not linear.

7. *Humility*

- Works to serve the group and the group's process of development; Trusts that the answers will come from the group, not from one's own knowledge

8. *A sense of humor, playfulness, and fun*

- Able to create an atmosphere that welcomes fun and encourages others to act with creativity and boldness

- Able to create an informal atmosphere that is interactive, relational and full of meaningful back and forth conversation with a friendly approach to serious issues

Not All Leaders Have Titles

During the MRSA infection prevention initiative at Billings Clinic, in Billings MT, staff members from multiple departments answered several survey questions, one of which simply asked with whom have you worked to prevent MRSA. A network map based on the answers showed an unexpected go-to person. A young oncology nurse had taken a special interest in the project. She researched medical sources on MRSA and interviewed nurse and physician colleagues experienced with diagnosing and treating it. She then made pocket cards with information caregivers could use for informing patients and answering questions. Her contacts with people outside her own unit made her a hub of connectivity, and a resource for the infection control team when they wanted to introduce new ideas. She also became an active participant in other, related initiatives.

Setting the Conditions for APD Success

Setting the conditions for the broadest community engagements is essential to generating ideas, experiences, questions, and answers from the usual and – most importantly – unusual suspects. The following suggestions open the doors, but remember, *Whoever shows up and wants to be involved are the right people.*

- Invite the whole community to the "launch."

- Invite informal and formal networks from the community. In a school system that would include departmental groups, division groups, ad hoc committees, special interest groups, teachers who are parents in the school, the PTA and even student groups.

- Consider how to accommodate everyone who wants to attend.

- Extend specific invitations to people to whom their peers turn to for advice, opinions, and help. The more people who are committed to the new initiative, the greater the likelihood for broad engagement within the community.

- Encourage participants with differing perspectives to enrich your group's interactions and ideas.

> Don't be buffaloed by experts and elites. Experts often possess more data than judgment. Elites can become so inbred that they produce hemophiliacs who bleed to death as soon as they are nicked by the real world.
>
> *– Colin Powell*

The following three examples illustrate of the richness of diverse perspectives:

1. A perfect example of broadening the circle was demonstrated when staff members at the Pittsburgh Veterans Hospital were discussing cleaning the room of a patient who had a C-diff (Clostridium Difficile) infection. One of the housekeepers said alcohol doesn't sterilize C-diff bacteria. He said Clorox was needed. Communication in hospitals usually travels along department lines and traditional hierarchies. Surprised, the infection control staff checked. They learned the housekeeper, who had studied chemistry, was right.

2. In one hospital infection prevention initiative, where all patients were supposed to have nasal swab tests for MRSA on admission and upon all moves from one hospital unit to another, the nursing staff was finding it difficult to keep track of when and whether tests had been done. The task became easier after a medical clerk suggested a pink slip on each bedside chart to show dates and locations of each test and the patient's MRSA status. The pink slips were a visual reminder for staff to test each newly transferred patient, send the swab to the lab, and update the record. They pink slips were also a quick way to view existing MRSA data.

3. In another medical center, a physical therapist began putting colored ribbons on each piece of equipment that had been sterilized for use by the next patient, and a secretary started the practice of regular sterilization for all phones and keyboards. A chaplain found a cleanable plastic cover for his Bible. In each case where the whole hospital community took part in infection control, the incidence of healthcare associated infections declined dramatically.

Generative Conversations

The APD improvement work is informed and shaped by continual formal and informal generative conversations. "Generative" conversations are a core process throughout the APD initiative and lead to the discovery of new ideas, behaviors and practices.

Conversations that generate discovery require:

- A community that is experiencing the challenge

- Time enough to allow meaningful ideas about possible changes to unfold

- Commitment of participants

- An appreciative mindset

- Mutual respect among participants

- Careful listening when differences are present

- Open, nonjudgmental attitude toward what others are saying

For example, the VA infection control staff listened closely to what the housekeeper told them, and learned he was correct. New cleaning procedures were adopted, and there was an even more important shift. Recognition of the housekeeper's previously unnoticed expertise contributed to an atmosphere of inclusion that encouraged staff members at every level to join an active effort to prevent infection.

You and I do not see things as they are. We see things as we are.
Herb Cohen

Generative Conversations:
Distress, Reflection, and Respect

The 130 members of the environmental services staff of a large organization were not happy. They thought managers were remote and unempathetic. Several people agreed not enough work was getting done, but they disagreed on who or what was to blame. Employees and managers practiced generative conversations as part of an initiative facilitated by Plexus Institute. The unit leader was dismayed to learn many staffers thought he was a micromanager who stifled their efforts at innovation. He reviewed their observations and began to evaluate how he supervised and gave instructions. One day a stranger in the building asked him for directions, then suddenly said "never mind" and walked away. The unit leader saw the man later and asked what had happened. "I saw the look on your face and figured you didn't want to be bothered," the person told him. The unit leader apologized and deepened his own introspection. When he described the uncomfortable incident to the staff, the story seemed to make everyone more self-aware. He said later that shift in perspective influenced the way they wrote their expectations of themselves, their co-workers and their managers and spoke to each other. Frequent discussions continued, and workflow and morale improved. "Perceptions and relationships need constant attention, and the process of working on them never ends," he said. "Perceptions are facts for the people who hold them, and people at all levels of an organization have to learn to talk to each other instead of around each other." The goal, he said, is to be "receptive, responsive, and respectful."

Deep listening in APD. Photo Credit: Sharon Benjamin

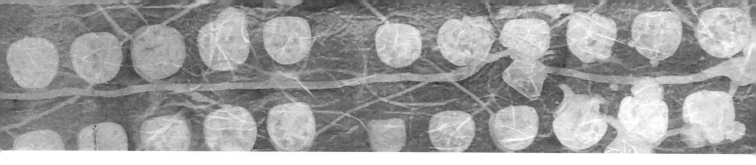

The Launch Event

The Launch Event

The Launch Event invites the whole community.
Active volunteers will emerge from the Launch Event, and they
will organize the Discover, Confirm, and Share phases and create
opportunities to imagine new possibilities.

The following ideas and practices are revisited throughout the APD process and provide a consistent guide for program design and facilitation.

The job of the facilitator is to be a spark plug who elicits the flow of ideas. Facilitator, as you prepare for the actual Launch Event, you can address these questions:

1. Why are we doing this?

2. Who should be invited?

3. Where should the Launch Event be held?

4. How should it be structured?

5. What happens next?

6. How will you know if you're off to a great start?

7. Review, reflect and track data

1. Why are we doing this?

Great ideas....come into the world quietly as doves. Perhaps then, if we listen attentively, we shall hear amid the uproar of empires and nations, the faint flutter of wings, the gentle stirrings of life and hope.
–Albert Camus

APD always starts with a clear, compelling, concrete, measurable problem, which, if solved, would have significant positive impacts. This is time to ask for and listen to compelling stories, the real cost of the problem to participants, and hope for the future.

2. Who should be invited?

The simple answer is *everyone*!

Everyone who might have an interest in the problem should be included in the invitation! Be creative with posters, announcements, displays, e-mails, word of mouth.

Be sure to invite those people who might be affected by a decision. This is especially powerful when you can bring together people who don't normally talk with one another. Bring together the people with information about the situation and lived experience with the situation in your group in order to articulate the problem and find solutions.

3. Where should the Launch Event be held?

Good Launch Events can be held in lobbies, cafeterias, or large open meeting rooms. Set up chairs to everyone can face one another. This conveys the essential message: "we are in this together, and we are working together."

4. How should it be structured?

Here is an example of a one-hour Launch Event agenda that you can adapt and use:

Time	What	Who	Supplies
5 minutes	Welcome, Thank you, Why we are here?	A leader in the system who cares about solving the problem	Microphone, flip chart, markers
12 minutes	1, 2, 4 - All (page 76)	All	
10 minutes	What do we know about the problem? Existing data? How it impacts us?*	A content expert	Charts, graphs, visuals
10 minutes	Stories** Giving a human voice to the problem. How does it impact our community?	Anyone (or several people) from the community	The Donkey Story (pg. 13) can be used if no group stories are available
10 minutes	How does this impact you?	In pairs or triads invite the audience to tell their stories.	
10 minutes	Invite some stories from the floor	Volunteers from the audience	
10 minutes	A new approach to a tough problem. Introduce APD, describe how it is different from "best practices." Tell Donkey Story.*	Leader	
10 minutes	Ideas about what we could do	All	Flip chart, markers
5 minutes	Here's how to get involved	Invite volunteers for a team to discover new ways of addressing the problem	Poster sign-up for next meeting giving the time, location and any instructions necessary

*Tell "The "Donkey Story," a Persian folktale. (on pg 13)

** Combine Stories and Statistics: We've found a personal story from one or more individuals who have been impacted by the problem is often sufficient to get the group ready to move into action. Stories and statistics will become increasingly important. As with data, keep a folder of samples, ideas, stories, and statistics that unfold over time.

5. What happens next?

At the end of the Launch Event meeting announce the date, time and place for the first project meeting and invite all people who are interested in solving the problem to attend. This first meeting for the team of interested volunteers is critically important. This is the meeting where you will organize your team and get started on Discovery and Action. There are guidelines in the next section of this guide for Discovery and Action Dialogues (DAD) that will support the facilitation of team meetings. Using several Liberating Structures in your first project team meeting will help you get off to a great start. See the appendices for ideas about Liberating Structures to use.

6. Organizing your team after the Launch Event

The composition of the volunteer team that comes together after the Launch Event will probably change over time. The emergent facilitator of this team will lead the team in creating the conditions for this team to be successful. The team needs to decide how often to meet, how to create a project plan and timeline, negotiate how responsibility will be divvied up, and decide when the next several meetings will be held to begin the project cadence. The team knows your organization best, so pay careful attention to the ideas and answers suggested by the group.

After the initial enthusiasm for APD has subsided, the facilitator's job may be to serve as the host and cheerleader for the team to keep energy and focus intact. APD teams in most organizations self-organize the agenda for the meeting of the team real-time at the beginning of each meeting. This is a good way of practicing nothing-about-me-without me (one of the Simple Rules). After a few team meetings, when information from DADs starts to pour in, the team may have to be more diverse to solve the problem. This is the time to recruit new people to the team, especially unusual suspects from different areas of the organization that don't normally participate. This is good news, and means that your organization is making progress.

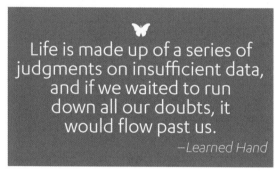

Life is made up of a series of judgments on insufficient data, and if we waited to run down all our doubts, it would flow past us.

—*Learned Hand*

7. How to know if you're off to a great start?

One of the most valuable outcomes during the Launch Event phase is the new data and participant feedback generated. Some things to keep track of include:

- How many people participated - in the Launch Event? In the first team meeting?

- Are a variety of roles, grade levels, staff, related arts, administrators represented? Did anyone surprising show up?

- Who is talking to whom?

- Is there anything different/ surprising about these combinations and conversations?

- Any new relationships developing?

- Who emerged as a real voice/ leader?

- Who volunteered for specific tasks, such as note taking.

- How were the conversations? Lively? Stilted?

- What topics were covered? Are there any patterns? Did topics build on each other and take unexpected directions?

- Were any subjects that are normally taboo brought up? How honest/authentic was the conversation about these topics?

- Was it clear that this work is palpably different from how your group normally operates? How do you know this?

8. Review, reflect, and track data

APD use measurable outcomes throughout the process; considering how you will assess/measure progress at the very beginning of the project establishes how the group will review, reflect and track data and milestones. You are invited to use multiple forms of data collection.

9. Reach out for support from other APD Practitioners

As you continue to work with the APD process within your organization, if you have questions and would like some guidance, Plexus Institute would be glad to connect you with consultants and practitioners who have used APD successfully. Reach out, if you want some seasoned advice or are feeling stuck. And, because initial conditions matter, reaching out early to get support can help you avoid losing traction later.

What Happens After the Launch Event

APD is an emergent, spiraling process. Questions and activities can and will be revisited throughout the entire APD process as the team works through ideas to address the problem/challenge. The process spirals through these phases

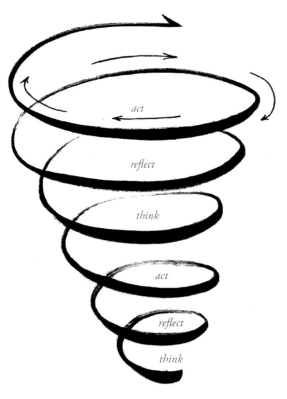

- Launch

- Discover, Confirm, Share

- Repeat Discover, Confirm, Share

- Repeat Discover, Confirm, Share

The true measure of success is learning and change at the individual level and the systems level. An "unfinished" project may, for example, stimulate ideas for others and be useful in different contexts. The core of APD is a reflective inquiry approach, in which every turn of the spiral influences a potential transformation of practice. Through every cycle, a deeper understanding of the issue, the nature of change, and potential creative responses evolve from critical reflective learning.

Group Reflection at this Point in Process

In the days after launching this work, there are additional things for your volunteer team to notice. These can be important to help shape and shift what you're doing to ignite, support and extend problem solving. This could include evaluating:

- Oops, are we shifting into expert problem-solver mode?

- Is your list of to-do's getting longer? If your list is growing longer, how can it become our list?

- Have we made time to ask who has some energy/passion to investigate, work on, and have a conversation about an element of the problem?

- Are we getting the resources we need? Meeting time and rooms, release time for staff, and meeting supplies are all resources that can be in high demand.

- Are we being invited to share what's happening in other department or organizational meetings?

- Are peers, colleagues, and formal leaders supporting one another and the process?

- Do the people showing up for our follow-up team meetings represent diverse roles including some "unusual suspects?"

Remember the value of revisiting Core APD questions

- What do you *know* about the problem?

- What do you *do* about the problem?

- What gets in the way of doing what you know you should and want to do to address the problem? What stops you from doing it every time?

- Do you notice anyone who seems to be successfully overcoming these barriers? Who? What are they doing differently?

- Who else should we be asking about this problem or that idea?

- Finally, who wants to volunteer for the next step?

Catching Butterflies — Your New Job

Capturing butterflies was the phrase coined by one of the APD/MRSA coordinators in the first round of hospitals using APD – He said: "I used to know my job – it was to tell people important things. Now, my job is harder because I spend all my time trying to capture butterflies." (Source: D. Hares, AEMC)

And in fact, that's exactly right — the most important thing a facilitator can do is to notice and capture the butterflies. Butterflies are those lovely, often small ideas that someone will float into a conversation. These ideas are often either so small, or so obvious, that we in regular practice frequently fail to capture them, because we don't explicitly notice them. When we don't explicitly notice these butterflies, we miss an opportunity to turn them from ideas into action.

Everyone's job is to capture those butterflies –

When you think a butterfly is floating around but hasn't been made explicit, here are some good prompts to use to help capture it:

- Wow, did you guys just notice that..........?

- Can you repeat that?

- What do you all think about ....?

Discover Phase

Keep an eye out for unexpected gifts with curiosity and interest in other people's perspectives, curiosity about the issue itself, and commitment to the evolving collaborative process.

The Discover phase is the fulcrum of APD. The whole APD process revolves around exploring and discovering ideas and solutions that are sometimes hidden in plain sight and sometimes exist in latent form but need to be nudged into becoming "real" and available to all. In the Discover Phase, it is important to consider *attributes* and *orientations* that fuel *discovery*.

The big shifts in attributes and orientation required during the Discover phase include moving from

- expert to explorer;

- telling to asking;

Why do some people donate organs, while neighbors don't?

A difference, more clerical than cultural, had huge impact

Behavioral Economist Daniel Ariely studied differences in organ donation in several European Countries in which organ donation choices accompanied drivers' licenses. Denmark and Sweden are culturally similar, yet the percentage of people willing to donate their organs after death differed vastly—only 4.25 percent in Denmark, and 85.9 percent in Sweden. In Austria 99.98 percent of drivers were willing donors, while in Germany only 12 percent were. Yet Austria and Germany share many cultural similarities. What accounted for the differences? It turned out the difference was clerical, more than cultural, but the impact was huge. The countries with low levels of donation asked people to "opt in" on their drivers' licenses—meaning they have to check a box to indicating their willingness to donate. Countries with high levels of potential donors had an "opt out." That meant you'd be automatically enrolled in a donor program unless you checked the box to decline.

Why did that small change matter so much? The decision itself isn't small. What happens to our bodies after death is a highly emotional matter, and the choice will affect people close to us. Ariely (http://danariely.com/2008/05/05/3-main-lessons-of-psychology/) suggests we tend not to like thinking about it. When we're uncertain on difficult issues we choose the default option, Ariely writes. He adds that physicians choose default options making medical decisions, and so do people making investment and retirement decisions. So examining default positions and small changes that influence them is a big deal.

- following orders to taking initiative;

- seeing problems to seeing possibilities;

- knowing to learning;

- routine to innovation;

- best-practice solutions to participant-discovered solutions; and

- big, sweeping initiatives to small, local changes.

> You do not need to know precisely what is happening, or exactly where it is all going. What you need is to recognize the possibilities and challenges offered by the present moment, and to embrace them with courage, faith, and hope.
> —Thomas Merton

These shifts sound reasonable, but can be very difficult to effect and maintain because many of us are highly rewarded for becoming "experts" in our work and in our organizations. To assume the posture of being a learner requires a deep shift in our orientation and willingness to take risks. These risks are substantial and may include appearing not to know, acknowledging that we don't know, asking for help, and disregarding the temptation to tell others what we know.

Just as when we travel to a new geographical location, becoming a good explorer and discoverer requires an attitude adjustment — and a change in how we look, hear, sense, and understand what's happening.

If the APD work feels like it is getting stuck, the team can do a quick check to see if everyone is still working in discovery mode. In addition to the attributes and orientations required for the process of discovery, it is important to ask the core APD questions again (listed below) to elicit fresh and innovative results. When used with fidelity and clear intention, these questions move the APD process forward.

> The greatest obstacle to discovering the shape of the earth, the continents, and the oceans was not ignorance but the illusion of knowledge.
> —Daniel J. Boorstin

Core APD Questions

These questions are important to keep in mind throughout the process. As a reminder, they should be asked as presented here and in the order presented below, and then revisited over and over again so that the community stays on track during each phase of the APD process. These question provide your organizing structure.

- What do you *know* about the problem?

- What do you *do* about the problem?

- What gets in the way of doing what you know you should and want to do to address the problem? What stops you from doing it every time?

- Do you notice anyone who seems to be successfully overcoming these barriers? Who? What are they doing differently?

- And, very important: Who else should we be asking about this problem or that idea?

- Finally, who wants to volunteer for the next step?

These questions form the backbone of your APD process. And, there are many ways of asking these questions. One way is through the Discovery and Action Dialogues, which are discussed next, and there are myriad other ways to use these same questions with your group. Some examples include the chocolate pudding story and the Jasper Palmer video, both discussed earlier in this book. The way in which you ask these questions is limited only by your imagination: role playing, simple ethnography, and 1-2-4-All are all ways of engaging people with the core APD questions. For more information on these techniques, please refer to Liberating Structures.com/menu.

A straightforward and illuminating way to ask these core questions is called a Discovery and Action Dialogue.

Sharing what is being learned. Photo Credit: Sharon Benjamin

Discovery and Action Dialogues (DADs)

One of the most productive methods used in facilitating APD is the Discovery and Action Dialogue (DAD). DADs are one of many Liberating Structures. The group will identify what the ideal state is, what gets in the way of achieving that, and any successful practices that overcome the barriers that they all face. They'll decide whether any of those practices are worth trying for themselves, and then create an *action plan* for getting that process started.

How to do a DAD:

- Choose an informal environment. Standing meetings are fine, check-ins in the hallway or cafeteria, you don't have to sit for a DAD – they should be short, energetic exchanges – 12-20 minutes is a good length to aim for. Over 30 minutes is probably too long. As the facilitator, it is important to help the group chunk (see vocabulary) their conversations into short, **actionable**, small and large next steps.

- Establish a collegial atmosphere with casual conversation.

- Begin with the purpose of the conversation – "We're here to talk together about (the challenge) and learn about your experiences."

- Then initiate the series of structured DAD questions. Curiosity and questions drive the APD process; asking and reflecting generates new "answers."

Tips for facilitating a DAD

- Sit informally in a circle with the group. Or, stand for shorter conversations.

- Make eye contact with all as you speak.

- Use your body language to show interest while you are listening carefully.

- Watch for body language signifying excitement or discomfort and ask about it.

- Don't give advice.

- Use open-ended questions: "What, how, what if?"

- Model consistently saying "Yes, and…," then add a broad question and notice what happens.

- "Catch butterflies" – This is when you pick up on something sparkling people in the group have just said that seems useful and actionable. Use their actual words – *I think I just heard you say.* Ask the rest of the group about it – *What do you think about what was just said?* Choose multiple actions that they agree to do. Look for solutions or potential solutions that have been offered in dialogue or that emerged from the conversation.

- If people use absolutes (always, never), push back with light humor. You mean nobody ever/everybody always does…..? When they acknowledge the exception to that "rule" of always or never, the exception could be a candidate for a positively deviant practice. Someone is doing something differently that is worth looking at.

- Resist importing solutions that have worked in other places. Just because something worked in one place doesn't mean it will work in another. If someone suggests an idea that sounds like a best practice, ask the group: *What do you all think about that? Would that work here? How?*

- A key thing to remember about DADs is that whatever behaviors are identified as being worthy of trying are only "candidates" for making a positive difference. It's only after testing in the field and determining with some sort of data (qualitative or quantitative) that the outcomes have changed for the better that the practice will be deemed to be preferential. It also has to be a practice that others can do as well.

DADs are ultimately about actions. The heart of APD is that the community experiencing the challenge identifies practices "hidden in plain sight" from within their midst. Then, they try out the practices, and if they work, adopt them as their own.

Sometimes, APD helps people identify good ideas about behaviors that weren't already in place. Here are two examples:

1. Teachers in an urban school used APD to integrate academic language more fully into their work. A music teacher tried something new: he had students listen to a recording of their rendition of a song, then write a critique using all the academic words he listed. He said the essays were thoughtful, and their next music performance was the best ever.

2. A group of art educators from many different schools were trying to figure out how to improve the hand-off from the regular classroom teacher into their classes. One person said maybe it would help if we always greeted the incoming class at the door. People agreed and reported substantial improvement with just that small change.

APD helps us act our way into a new way of thinking about how to solve problems by finding existing solutions and imagining new actions to test.

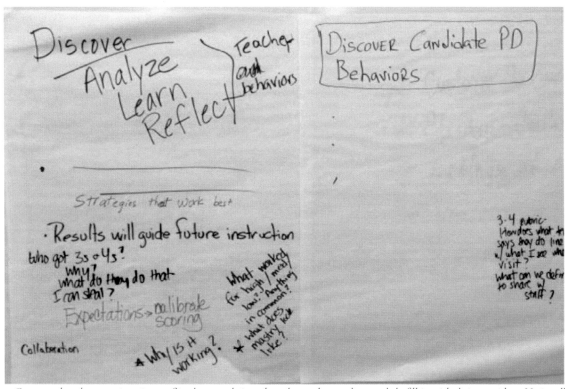

Capture what the group is saying on flip charts and give others the markers so they can help fill in with their own ideas. Notice all the different hand writing in this photo. Photo Credit: Mark Munger

How do you know if you are doing good Discovery and Action Dialogues?

We all want to know if we're doing a good job, especially when we're trying something new. If you find yourself wondering how you are doing as a DAD facilitator, after you've conducted 10 – 15 Discovery and Action Dialogues, stop and take a look at your personal To-Do list.

If you're doing effective DADs, as the facilitator, your own to-do list shouldn't be getting significantly larger or longer with action items for you to follow-up on. If you are conducting effective DADs, participants should be volunteering to take on new activities, play new roles and help remove barriers to better practice…..this is so true that you may find this shift disconcerting. If you find yourself wondering what you should be doing, you may be on exactly the right track! As participants begin to become active in solving problems by removing barriers, your job shifts from being the do-er to being the conductor or orchestrator.

Does this mean your job will get easier? Not necessarily, you may find that you have to work harder at running interference for newly engaged staff, you may find that you're doing more outreach and offering new and different invitations to usual and unusual suspects and, in what may be your biggest new role, you may have to pay much closer attention to small ideas – and the potential power that can be unleashed by lots and lots of small ideas turning into big change.

So, keep track of what's on everyone's to-do list – if your to-do list is the only one getting longer, you will have to rethink how you are asking and listening to the answers to the final core questions of APD:

Do you have any ideas? and

What could we do now? Are there any volunteers?

It Takes the Whole System to Find the Solution

At Einstein Hospital, while working to protect patients from hospital acquired infections, staff said that many patients need special precautions, and the door signs directing people entering their rooms to don some combination of gowns, gloves and masks, needed clarification. The issue of how to improve the signs came up repeatedly in DADs. Improving the signs was no small undertaking because to change the signs meant changing hospital policy and that meant including voices from Corporate Communications, Facilities Management, Housekeeping, Clinicians, Interior Designers, Quality Improvement staff and patients and families, along with the infection control staff. Shepherding proposals for new signs required the APD facilitators to pay attention, report on progress, solicit input, test alternatives and garner support all while keeping the sign issue moving forward. All told, changing the signs took over a year.

When the new signs were delivered, just before Christmas, the General Supply staff person making the deliveries said: "I've never seen anything like it! I should be wearing a Santa hat delivering these signs. People are so excited to get 'their' signs, everybody feels like they own the new signs, we're not going to have trouble getting these used."

Photo Credit: Susanne Salem-Schatz

Finally, ideas about possible solutions may be generated that require more systems-level engagement and work. These ideas are often not new but their solutions, while sometimes obvious, are solutions that require collaboration and agreement from many parts of the system. As the facilitator, you are responsible for nudging these ideas through the larger process, and reporting back frequently on your progress. When done well, and in conjunction with noticing and acting on small, local ideas, APD can create a great, symbiotic dynamic tension that can generate energy and sustain enthusiasm.

As you read in the section on your Launch Event and what happens immediately after you launch APD, your volunteer team is incredibly important. After you and colleagues have conducted several DADs, you will have lots and lots of ideas. Some of these ideas can be solved where they were initially brought up, but other ideas will have to go back to your volunteer team for discussion about possible solutions. Keeping your volunteer team as permeable as possible and regularly inviting in unusual suspects from across your organization will provide you with greater opportunities to solve problems in unexpected ways. For example, one organization discovered a barrier to good practice was that there was that the housekeeping staff was being asked to clean rooms in record times to reduce costs. People using the rooms were faced with wet surfaces because the cleaning products were slow drying. By inviting the head of housekeeping to the team, the issue was raised, discussed, and solved in a single meeting.

Additional Ways to Generate Ideas and Energy During the Discovery Phase

- **Consider the simple rule "Take 20 Seconds."** When you let silence linger until someone in the group volunteers a new idea, an in- sight, or a thought you are making room for additional contributions. Model the APD principle of "no right answers" by asking the assembled group good questions and then waiting for people in the group to answer. Pause for reflection after asking a question. Try posing the question and then waiting 20 seconds for someone else to speak. Twenty seconds of silence in a group can feel like a very long time – on average, facilitators begin speaking after 6 seconds – so, increase your tolerance of long pauses. During these long pauses people in the group are often formulating their answers and working up the courage to respond. One good way to encourage the group to respond is to quietly look around the group with a calm expression that signals this is time for reflection and thinking. It helps to focus attention on your own breathing. It helps to calm you, taking away pressure to begin talking. This strategy takes practice – and can be very effective.

- **Focus on assets that may not be recognized. Notice what's working.** Critical to a successful APD Launch is to focus on what's currently working. What are the practices that are working? What are the positive differences among us that work and how do we know? Keeping data is important, so that we know why. Will others be able to do the practices successfully?

- **Encourage and discover new voices and perspectives**. Listen to all voices, especially "unusual suspects." Refer to The Rule of Six shared on the following page.

- **Intentionally use words and phrases that communicate**:

  - **Trust** – we are certain that we will discover the solutions from within our midst.

  - **Honesty** – we are not committed to any pre-selected idea, and we are open to the solutions that emerge from the group.

  - **Curiosity** – we are eager to discover what solutions might emerge.

  - **Invitation** – we want anybody and everybody who'd like to participate to be a part of our improvement effort.

  - **Community** – we are working together to discover from within our community – a more positive outcome to our problem/challenge.

The Rule of Six: Encourage all voices and perspectives. Listen to all voices, especially unusual suspects.

When we are trying to figure out something perplexing, or when we are facing into uncertainty, it seems natural to our western way of thinking to quickly try to find the right answer to questions like this: "Exactly what is the cause of this? What's going on here? What is likely to happen? What should be our plan?" Many of the most heated arguments, whether within our own heads, or among colleagues or with family members, are about who has the one answer to the question before us.

The "rule of six," a Native American thinking process or discipline, requires that instead of coming up with one single answer to the question (which comes from the story we tell ourselves about what is going on), we instead come up with at least six possible, or good, stories about what is going on. And then having done that, we hold all six stories in mind, and do not immediately choose among them.

This is very hard for the Western mind. Even when we think of two possibilities, it is for the implicit purpose of having those two possibilities fight it out, until one wins. Thinking about more than one cause of an event or more than one possibility of an outcome is, in our minds, is simply an invitation for us to quickly choose the right one. In fact, we move so rapidly from what we observe, to the story that we tell ourselves about that observation, to a conclusion, that we hardly realize that there is a space between what we see and the story we tell ourselves about it. We go from perception to story to conclusion in a nanosecond.

The Native tradition, by contrast, holds that we can create a generous and open space in our minds after we notice something. In that space, we can hold many possible stories about the phenomenon, various interpretations and multiple perspectives on possible developments all in dynamic tension.

The ability to hold six possibilities in our mind accomplishes several things:

- It keeps our perceptions open to a wider range of data.

- It allows us to be "systems thinkers" seeking multiple roots of causality in multiple dimensions of a situation.

- It keeps folks from having a fight with each other about who is right at a time when they should be listening with curiosity to why each other sees things differently.

Since we are not forcing ourselves to invest our ego in a single best idea, we can be more flexible in our thinking. If our personal favorite possibility isn't shown to be the strongest in the unfolding of data, we can more easily shift our emotional commitment to another idea, which in the course of time has proved stronger; and, we can make that shift earlier and more easily.

The rule of six allows us to make necessary decisions, yet remain aware and realistic, more flexible in our thinking, present to the world and to the thoughts and perceptions of others, and perhaps even more compassionate with ourselves.

When you are in the Discovery phase of APD, you may experiment the asking yourself, the leadership group and participants. "What is another possible story, cause, interpretation, perception to describe what is happening?" Do this, until you have six possible stories, or six plausible causes, or six useful directions in which to proceed. Then, let those possibilities sit in everyone's mind until the next meeting; resist trying to come to a conclusion or consensus at the same meeting where possibilities are explored (adapted from www.judysorumbrown. com, *A Leader's Guide to Reflective Practice*).

Moving Toward the Confirm and Share Phases

- The group is using data and dialogue that reveal possibly different and better practices that are happening.

- Practices in action are becoming clear and the group believes that the practices are those they'd like to try for themselves.

- The group has tapped into multiple potential sources of expertise about potentially different and more successful practices. For example, In a hospital initiative to improve pain management with APD processes, nurses in medical wards discovered they had untapped expertise nearby. Nurses in the post-anaesthesia care unit (PACU) understood powerful medicines that floor nurses generally didn't use, and pharmacists, whose unit was staffed 24 hours, were eager to help. PACU nurses and pharmacists brought new knowledge and experience to the pain project, and people who hadn't previously met began collaborating with new enthusiasm on improved strategies.

> The age old art of story is one of the MOST effective tools leaders can use. But [we] need to pick [our] stories carefully and match them to the situation.
> — *Steve Denning*

- Group members have engaged with usual and unusual suspects.

- The group has collected data from individuals using practices associated with effective outcomes.

- Home-grown stories that capture the essence of the problem and the behaviors that are leading to effective outcomes have been expressed in the DADs and elsewhere.

Unexpected solution from unusual suspects

After the launch of a new infection control initiative at the Hospital El Tunal in Bogota, Colombia, a group of uniformed security guards joined workers from other hospital departments at a voluntary meeting. During a discussion of hand hygiene, the guards saw a new opportunity to contribute, and an APD practice was born. They began distributing sanitizing hand gel to everyone who entered the external hospital entrances and all who entered the internal entrances to nursing units. In a decisive statement about the importance of clean hands, they called it holy water. The idea caught on, and the label was widely used throughout the hospital community (Singhal, Buscell, & Lindberg, 2010).

Confirm and Share Phases

APD starts with a problem that is concrete. Progress towards solving the problem involves noticing and concretely measuring behaviors and practices.

APD works best when the people in the community are involved in deciding what measures make sense to them, what they are already paying attention to, and what subtle measures they have been using all along. Data to assess progress can be generated in many ways. Keeping track of emerging patterns and trends in behavior and practice, whether positive or negative, is critical to the overall understanding of APD in practice. This process involves vetting stories, tracking outcomes, and noting successful solutions. The responsibility for noticing and making sense of data belongs, rightly, to everyone in the community.

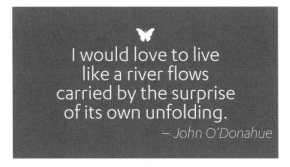

I would love to live
like a river flows
carried by the surprise
of its own unfolding.
— John O'Donahue

Confirm with Data

Considerations and guidelines for continuous data gathering are an important tool for sharing with the entire community.

1. Rather than looking for cause and effect (which can be difficult to prove), APD processes focus on finding behaviors that are associated with (correlated with) improvements. Looking for useful correlations between behaviors and outcomes is the most productive way to discover solutions for the problem.

2. The manipulation of physical materials within a group often opens doorways to creativity and innovation. In groups, and together, practice creating visual methods of displaying data using poster board, chart paper, colored markers, yarn, stickers, or popsicle sticks. Collect some fun data, such as birthdays of each member of the group.

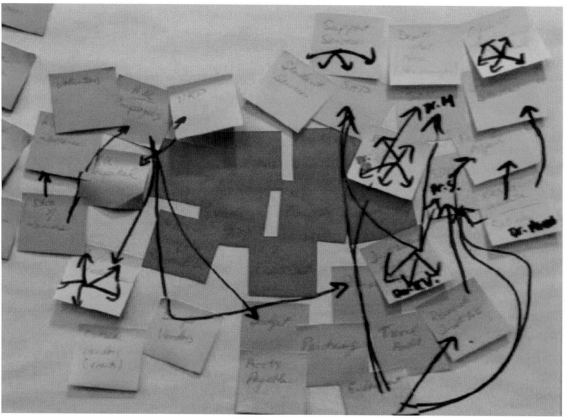

A social network map for a new initiative – color-coded by person and job type. Photo Credit: Sharon Benjamin

3. Use "Run Charts" for tracking data. See the section on Run Charts below.

4. Keep track of various types of data. In groups, find a self-appointed or volunteer archivist who enjoys collecting and maintaining new records. This material can be reviewed for spotting and analyzing trends. Often notes of gatherings yield good insights when reexamined for trends and "A-ha" moments. For example, in one international service provider organization, the scribe for a meeting was transcribing the notes of the discussion and realized that two principals were using the same word to mean two very different things. At the next meeting the group could openly discuss and resolve the tension by clarifying what was actually intended.

5. Keep an eye out for what might be "hidden in plain sight." (Review The Donkey Story in the Launch section of this guide). Use APD processes to make explicit the small behaviors that fuel

higher performance. Encourage the community to look for and recognize the sometimes hard-to-see solutions that might be resulting in small (or large) innovations and success.

6. Look for and invite unusual suspects to get involved. These are people within the community who might have information, insight, knowledge, experience, and wisdom.

7. The community will own and value the data if they collect and analyze it themselves.

Observation and Information from an Unusual Suspect: A Thrilling Example of Life-saving Action

Bob was an experienced pilot and had focused his academic research on cockpit teams, and how they make mistakes that result in crashes. His research uncovered a finding that almost anytime a plane crashed, the knowledge required to avert the crash was present "within the skin of the plane," but nobody paid attention.

Sometimes, it was a passenger who spotted something wrong. What would a passenger know? It's only a passenger - an unusual suspect! The ultimate tale of a passenger being ignored was the experience of an engineer who had helped to design the supersonic Concorde, which had a history of blowing tires. One day, this senior engineer was settling back into his seat as the plane rolled down the runway for take-off. He heard a tire blow, and seated by the wing window, he looked out as a metal shard thrown from the wheel pierced the wing and the fuel tank and jet fuel began to stream out. He hit the call button. The flight attendant came, and he described what he'd seen; she said, "sit down and buckle your seatbelt." He ignored her and ran for the cockpit and began pounding on the door. The co-pilot came to the door and ordered the distressed engineer to go back to his seat, sit down, and buckle his seatbelt. The distressed engineer knew that his life and the life of everyone on the plan was at stake, so he grabbed the co-pilot by his lapels and dragged him down the aisle to hold his face against the window where he could see the stream of jet fuel pouring out of the wing. The co-pilot immediately ran back to the cockpit, and the Concorde did a tight turn back toward the airport where it landed safely.

Judy Brown (2006) reflects in A Leader's Guide to Reflective Practice. "If a big strapping, experienced, senior male engineer, who helped design the plane, can't get heard, what hope is there for the rest of us - for the younger, slightly confused, uncertain people who might hold the critical piece of information that could save our lives?" We have an essential stewardship responsibility to create the conditions for conversations that get critical perspectives voiced and listened to, even if we appear to be seeing different things.

Transparency and Integrity

During the Confirm phase the community determines if practices that appear to be making a positive difference are "available to all." What does "available to all" mean?

1. No special skills are required – what works well can be learned and accomplished by everyone.

2. The better results can be obtained in multiple different environments – the outcomes are a result of practice, not the context or individual personalities.

3. No extraordinary resources are needed – the better results can be obtained using materials that everyone already has or has access to

The third point above is relatively easy to determine. However, the other two require a determination on the part of the individual and the community regarding the process itself. How will you know? Ask yourself:

*   Is the process being learned and replicated with fidelity in different environments?

*   If learning a new behavior, is the behavior clear? Have others tried out the behavior? Have you given each other feedback? Tried again? Clarified? Tried again?

*   Can observers see that the behavior is successful, even if changes are made to suit local conditions?

In order to answer questions like this the qualities of integrity and transparency are necessary. Integrity requires a disciplined look at what is being done and asking questions like:

*   If I'm honest with myself, have I worked to learn how to do the new practice well?

*   Am I confident enough using the new behavior that I can adjust and monitor for my present situation while keeping the intent and characteristics of the behavior?

*   If I'm using the practice with fidelity, am I truly getting different and better outcomes?

Transparency is necessary to talk honestly about what is happening and why. If everyone shares stories of their ideas, struggles, setbacks, successes, and learnings, then others will be attracted to engage in the work.

Clarify with Paradox: Both/And and Complementary Pairs

As the community moves through the Confirm and Share phases, everyone might be grappling with information that challenges long-held beliefs. People might be asking each other, "How can this be true, if something different is happening over here?" People may be experiencing high levels of dynamic tension.

Paradox in the APD process is useful: *rather than choosing one idea or the other, hold both in your thoughts and actions simultaneously.* Sometimes this is referred to as creating dynamic tension. Holding the paradox while asking a question like, "How can we create a curriculum that works for the entire class and meets each student's individual needs?" can stimulate new ways of thinking about the challenge and lead to approaches that are different from the usual ones. Ask

- What are the challenges you face?

- What kind of question can you create that challenges you to tackle both/and simultaneously?

Visual Approaches to Sharing Data

1. Run Charts – Tracking data: How do we know we've changed?

Run charts are an important tool for your APD work because, in order to assess change, think about how you will know if practices have changed and outcomes have improved. If a change isn't "moving the needle," then look at how you're doing what you're doing, and try something else.

In standard research and traditional quality improvement initiatives, data are usually collected prior to and following the intervention (pre and post assessments). In APD, measuring outcomes throughout the process is important. One way to measure improvement on a continuous basis is to use run charts.

Run charts display active data graphically *over a period of time* to determine if a process is changing, or not. All outcomes can be thought of as *processes*. For instance, the outcome "students who are college-ready" can be thought of as "the process of educating students so that they're college ready."

It's useful to have a baseline period with measurements before your interventions take place. Think of your travel to work as an example. If you left for work at exactly the same time every day and measured the time from leaving your home to arriving at your workplace there would be variability in those times. The reason for those variations could include traffic, weather, holidays, accidents, or road construction. Some of these will be more predictable than others. For instance, if it's likely that a holiday is going to have a major impact on your travel time, you might choose to change your normal habit to some other time.

Other variables, like the impact of normal traffic and timing of the traffic lights, typically can't be predicted in advance. The way these variables come together day after day to impact your outcome results in a range of expected outcomes. Some days the lights are all green and you get to work earlier than expected. Other days the person in front of you drives eight miles an hour below the speed limit, and you get to work later than expected. You can determine what your average time is, and you can be quite certain what the range of possibilities is likely to be (barring special cause events like accidents or weather). From one day to the next, you can't predict in advance where within the range you'll be. The range of these normal day-to-day variations form your base line.

In order to impact a process so that change occurs, you need to do something different. Continuing with our example – if you leave the house at the same time and travel to the same place each day, what are the things you could do to change the process of getting to work, so that it's quicker? Pick a different route; use a different, faster, smaller vehicle; try public transportation. Or, you could try a special cause solution, such as leaving for work at a different time, hoping to find different and more favorable traffic conditions.

Florence Nightingale: Heroic Nurse and Pioneer of Statistical Graphics

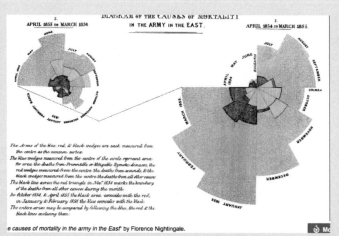

The Coxcomb, also called the Rose Diagram

In 1854 Florence Nightingale brought a team of 38 volunteer nurses to the Scutari military hospital to help care for British soldiers sounded in the Crimean War. She was shocked by what she found. The hospital, located in what is Istanbul today, lacked every essential—medicines, linens, basins, soap and clean clothing. And it was filthy, crawling with bugs and infested with vermin. She was also horrified to realize that ten times more men died of disease—such as typhus, cholera, and dysentery—than died from battle wounds. More than 4,000 men died her first winter there. She invented a mapping technique called the coxcomb, or the rose diagram, that showed dramatically, in color, how many soldiers died on a monthly basis from disease and how many died from wounds of war. She championed cleanliness and sanitation and campaigned for supplies to make that possible. She used her novel circular visual presentation to pressure Queen Victoria and governmental officials to act to save lives. Her work brought national attention to the field of public health, and she was one of the first medical practitioners in Europe to grasp the power of the new field of statistics (Fee and Garofalo, 2011, and https://en.wikipedia.org/wiki/Florence_Nightingale).

The Areas of the blue, red, and black wedges are each measured from the centre as the common vertex.

The blue wedges measured from the centre of the circle represent area for area the deaths from Preventable or Mitigable Zymotic diseases, the red wedges measured from the centre the deaths from wounds, and the black wedges measured from the centre the deaths from all other causes.

The black line across the red triangle in Nov. 1854 marks the boundary of the deaths from all other causes during the month.

In October 1854, & April 1855, the black area coincides with the red, in January & February 1856, the blue coincides with the black.

The entire areas may be compared by following the blue, the red, and the black lines enclosing them (https://commons.wikimedia.org/wiki/File:Nightingale-mortality.jpg).

2. Creating a Run Chart

As you're trying interventions, collect data to determine usefulness.

- Start with the baseline, historical data.

- Then plot the data graphically, such as on an excel spreadsheet.

- Calculate a median for the data set and display that horizontally, as well.

- Make the x-axis reflect time.

- Make the y-axis reflect the amounts of whatever you're measuring, as time passes.

For example, in the Run Chart below, the x-axis represents the school year week-by-week, and the y-axis represents weekly math quiz scores.

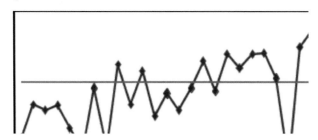

(Balestracci, 2009)

Each individual or group of consecutive data points that are above or below the median (red line) is called a "run." A run ends each time the line crosses the median to a new data point. (Points that fall exactly on the median don't count as part a run.) On the chart above, how many runs do you see? The correct answer is 10.

The characteristics of the runs will determine if the data reflects random variation, normal variation within the baseline range, or shows a true shift in the process. If *you have six or more consecutive points on the same side of the median, that is indicative of a true shift in the process.* Do you see any true shifts on the above graph? Yes - there are two. In the beginning, at the left side of the data, there was a shift - the first 8 data points are below the median. That means that, at that time, performance was lower than average. This is not a value judgment – lower may be better. The second shift is at the end, on the right side of the data set. The final 9 points are all above the median, meaning the current process is reliably producing higher outcomes.

Any run chart should have at least 12 data points, so frequent data collections are important. 18-30 data points are ideal, and any more than that is unnecessary. As you add more data, eliminate the earlier points from your display, so that you have a constant 18-30 data points. As new data are entered, are the "runs" jumping from one side of the median to the other? If so, despite your intervention, your process is staying the same, at least in terms of outcomes produced. (The new traffic routes may be no better or worse than the original.) If, however, the data points start to be consistently on one side of the median or the other (at least 6 times in a row), then you know that the new behavior has changed the process significantly. Has the change resulted in improvement – in reliably positive outcomes? If so, it is an adaptive positive deviance that's making a difference!

It is useful in the APD process to prominently display one or more run charts that reflect the outcomes the community is looking to change. The run charts show whether the change is occurring, or not. When there is a real change for the better, celebrate it! When the intervention doesn't result in the desired improvement, then have a conversation about what everyone has learned and design another intervention, based on a new hypothesis. Use run charts to help make the invisible visible – one of the core tenets of APD.

Considerations for Choosing the Right Kind of Graph

1. Bar Graphs

Use a bar graph (horizontal or vertical bars) when you want to represent a simple comparison of data or show change over time. Bar graphs are useful for displaying

- activity of one thing through time, e.g. number of books each student reads per week,

- several categories of results at once, e.g. number of absences and number of hall passes each day in each grade, or math test scores of new students and returning students.

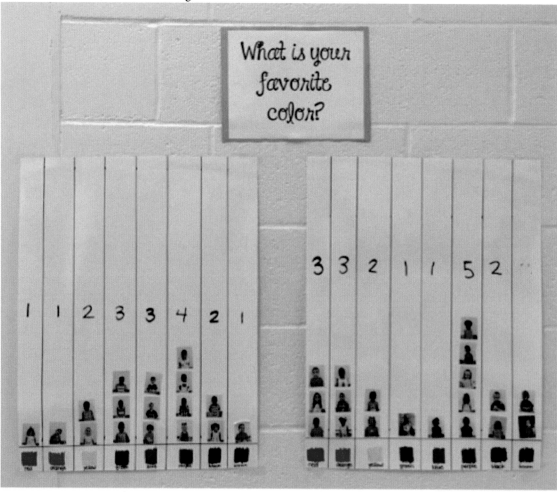

A memorable display of data Photo Credit: Laura Gardner

2. Line Graphs

Use a line graph to show sets of data points plotted over a time period, connected by straight lines. Line graphs are used to track changes over short and long periods of time.

When smaller changes exist, line graphs are better to use than bar graphs. Line graphs can be used to compare changes over the same period of time for more than one group (using two or more lines) in the same chart.

Line graphs are useful for displaying

- any set of figures that needs to be shown over time;

- results from two or more groups compared over time; and

- data trends over time.

Do not use a line graph if there are too many data points, small variations in values, or values that jump from very small to very large.

3. Pie Charts

Pie charts can quickly show proportions in relation to a whole, with each wedge representing a percentage of the total rather than raw numbers.

Pie charts are useful for displaying: (a) component parts of a whole in percentages and (b) budget, geographic, or population analysis.

Do not use a pie chart if there are too many divisions making it difficult to label and read. If possible, limit the number of divisions to eight or less.

Share what you are learning as you confirm

Critically important variables are: Who is sharing? How it is being shared? What is being shared?

Sharing clear evidence confirms the discovery of successful practices that are yielding different and better outcomes.

- Be sure to share the small ideas and subtle behaviors that might be making a difference.

- Share accuracy and validity of the discoveries, and their potential utility.

- Share when there are still opportunities for everyone to learn, explore, and discover or create other practices that can help achieve even better outcomes.

Who shares and how?

It is important for the APD team to share data with the community through regular touch points and meetings intentionally creating a consistent, ongoing pattern of communication. Bulletin boards, and other visual displays of information fuel APD work and conversation. Think about how to visualize data in exciting ways that invite others to share their own progress. The following ways have all been used to great effect in sharing APD progress:

- Colorful graphs using paint, macaroni, and beans – an effective, inexpensive, way to show how much;

- Photographs of the project team in action, especially photos that include unusual participants;

- Run charts displayed in central locations can be annotated with pictures to make clear the connection between what is happening and who is making it happen;

- Bulletin boards that post the DAD questions and have sticky notes and places for people to write responses.

All around us we see magnificent structure— galaxies, cells, ecosystems, human beings—that have somehow managed to assemble themselves.

– Steven Strogatz

In addition to the data being generated, it's important to also collect stories – including the stories of the process.

- Stories can be shared by the APD team in newsletters, blog posts, tweets, and Positive Gossip (a Liberating Structure that encourages people to share stories that are positive about the work being done.).

- Sharing can also be in the form of fun games, Youtube's, songs, artifacts, and other creative activities.

- Sharing can take place during in-service days, regularly scheduled meetings, special "flash mob" style meetings, and informally in the form of Positive Gossip (See Liberating Structures for how to use this technique).

Keep track of how many unusual suspects the APD team is reaching – this is a key indicator that the process of sharing is reaching all of the intended groups.

Thoughts on Closing...

Applied Positive Deviance projects unfold differently in each community, and APD initiatives comes to embody the collective values and qualities of the people who tackle their most urgent challenges using APD processes. All APD projects, in the words of PD Pioneer Jerry Sternin, are bathed in data, and communities develop their own ways of meaningful measurement. In one hospital infection prevention initiative, staff members expended great energy gathering, refining and analyzing lab and medical data, and the numbers were rooted in the team's intellects and in their hearts. Fluctuations brought pain or joy, depending on whether each new set of figure indicated improvement, status quo, or a decline in outcomes.

In another healthcare organization with the same mission, instead of number crunching, staff members placed more emphasis on improvisation, acting out scenarios that brought problems, possibilities and relational issues to the surface. That too, generated data, often in the form of new questions. The improvs were fun, but always with a serious purpose. Teachers and administrators in schools with differing student populations explored existing, and newly gathered, data and experimented with their own unique ways to improve attendance, graduation rates, and learning breakthroughs.

Despite these contextually diverse initiatives, common themes emerged.

People collaborating across hierarchical and departmental boundaries on organizational teams deepened their understanding of their own jobs and developed more empathy and willingness to help people doing different kinds of work. Several participants reported changed human relationships and improved workplace culture, with more enthusiasm for the purpose of their work and more respectful communications. More people addressed each other by name. People who had never met could learn from each other using simple conversational structures. People trading tips for helpful practices tapped into a newly realized vein of generosity. People caught butterflies and celebrated small wins.

In one school, a teacher felt relieved to find a way to help students after a crossing guard told her the dangerous route they had to walk. Infection control specialists and school administrators said they were happy to be newly viewed as resources, rather than bearing their past reputation as enforcers. People shared goals, encouraged each other through frustrations, and found joy in successes. A group of nurses from one hospital pored over statistics on the dramatic decline in infections and infection-related mor-

tality that resulted from their hand-hygiene and infection prevention initiative. One nurse, with tears in her eyes, was struck by the deep meaning of their work: because of their efforts, there were patients who went home to their lives and families who would otherwise have died.

Not every APD project will save lives. But, when people in communities share commitment to a goal, have the processes and tools to work toward achieving that goal, when they approach the work together with an open mind and generosity of spirit, the possibilities for constructive, and surprising, outcomes are virtually unlimited. Unexpected gifts are no longer hidden in plain sight, but become available and useful.

Adaptive Positive Deviance is a set of guidelines and a process for helping groups work together to make meaningful improvements. We at Plexus Institute believes that any group can implement APD by asking questions, including everyone who cares, collecting data to prove what is happening, adjusting, adapting and applying what has been learned and repeating these steps again and again and again. We've seen it in action and we know it works. We've written this book to support you in your important work.

We hope this guide helps you get your Adaptive Positive Deviance work off to a great start. We invite you to share stories, experiences, data, and insights so that what you discover becomes available, too. For more ideas and support, please reach out to Plexus Institute at www.plexusinstitute.org.

References

Adams, M. *Question thinking, using questions for great results everywhere it matters.* www.inquiryinstitute.com.

Ariely, D. (2010). *Predictably irrational, revised and expanded edition: The hidden forces that shape our decisions.* New York: Harper Perennial.

Ariely, D. (2008). http://danariely.com/2008/05/05/3-main-lessons-of-psychology/

Balestracci, D. (2009). *Data sanity: A quantum leap to unprecedented results.* MGMA.

Block, P. (2003). *The answer to how is yes.* San Francisco: Berrett-Koehler.

Block, P. (2008). *Community: The structure of belonging.*

Boorstin, D. J., (1993). *The creators: A history of heroes of the imagination.* New York: Vintage.

Brown, J. (2006). *A leader's guide to reflective practice.* Victoria, Canada: Trafford Publishing.

Brown, Judy website www.judysorumbrown.com

Buchanan, M. (2007). *The social atom: Why the rich get richer, cheaters get caught, and your neighbor usually looks like you.* New York: Bloomsbury USA.

Buchanan, M. (2013). *Forecast: What physics, meteorology, and the natural sciences can teach us about economics.* New York: Bloomsbury USA Publishing.

Cabane, O. F., & Pollack, J. (2017). *The net and the butterfly: The art and practice of breakthrough thinking.* New York: Penguin Random House.

Camus, A. (1962). The artist and his time. *Modern Language Quarterly, 23*(2): 129-134. www.azer.com/aiweb/categories/topics/Quotes/quote_camus.html

Carse, J. (2003). *Varieties of ethical reflection.* Lanham, MD: Lexington Books

Cohen, H. (1982). *You can negotiate anything.* Bantam Books: New York.

Harbottle, T. B. (Ed.). (1906). Demosthenes Ad Leptinum 162. *Dictionary of Quotations (Classical.* New York: The Macmillan Co. Limited.

Denning, S. (2004). Telling tales. *Harvard Business Review, 82*(5):122-9, 152.

Dizikes, P. (2011). When the butterfly effect took flight. MIT Technology Review, Feb. 22, 2011. www.technologyreview.com/s/422809/when-the-butterfly-effect-took-flight

Easton, D. & Solow, L. (2016). *Complexity works! Influencing pattern-based change in teams and organizations.* www.complexityspace.com.

Fee, E. & Garofalo, M. E. (2011). *Florence Nightingale and the Crimean War.* /www.ncbi.nlm.nih.gov/pmc/articles/PMC2920984/

Greene, M. (2001). *Variations on a blue guitar.* New York: Teachers College Press.

Harmon, A. (2017). *Obstacle for climate science: Skeptical, stubborn students.* https://www.nytimes.com/2017/06/04/us/education-climate-change-science-class-students.html

Heifetz, R. A.(1994). Leadership without easy answers, *The Belknap Press of Harvard University Press.* Cambridge, MA.

Housden, R. (2001). *Ten poems to change your life.* New York: Harmony Books.

Intrator, S. M., & Scribner, M. (Eds.) (2014). *Teaching with Heart.* San Francisco: Jossey-Bass.

Intrator, S. M., & Scribner, M. (Eds.) (2007). *Leading from within.* San Francisco: Jossey-Bass.

Johnson, S. (2007). *The ghost map: The story of London's most terrifying epidemic--and how it changed science, cities, and the modern world.* New York: Riverhead Books.

Kelly K. (1994). *Out of control, The new biology of machines, social systems and the economic world.* Cambridge, MA: Perseus Books.

Kelso, J. A. S. & Engstrom, D. (2006). *The complementary nature.* Cambridge, MA: The MIT Press.

Kimball, L. (2012). Liberating structures: New pattern language for engagement. *The Systems Thinker, Pegasus Communications, Inc., Vol. 23 No. 1.*

Levitt, S. (2013). www.fastcompany.com/1683190/economist-steven-levitt-on-why-data-needs-stories

Lewin, K. (1943). Psychology and the process of group living. *Journal of Social Psychology,* 17, 113–131.

Liberating Structures website http://www.liberatingstructures.com

Lipmanowicz, H., & McCandless, K. (2013). *The surprising power of liberating structures: Simple rules to unleash a culture of innovation.* www. liberatingstructures.com

Merton, T. The Thomas Merton Center at Bellarmine University Home Page. http://merton.org/Roots/

Oliver, M. (2008). *Red bird.* Boston: Beacon Press.

Owen, H. http://www.openspaceworld.com

Palmer, P. J. Center for Courage and Renewal, Seattle, WA. www.couragerenewal.org/parker

Plexus Institute website www.plexusinstitute.org/blogpost/656763/170412/Power-of-Positive-Feedback-Often-MIssed?hhSearchTerms=%22positive+and+feedback%22&terms= T

Schein, E. (2013). *Humble inquiry: The gentle art of asking instead of telling.* San Francisco: Berrett-Koehler.

Schon, D. (1987). *Educating the reflective practitioner.* San Francisco: Jossey-Bass.

Senge, P. (2006). *Handbook of action research.* Thousand Oaks, CA: Sage.

Singhal, A., Buscell, P., & Lindberg, C. (2010). *Inviting everyone: Healing healthcare through positive deviance.* Bordentown, NJ: Plexus Press.

Srogatz, S. (2003). *Sync: How order emerges from chaos in the universe.* New York: Hyperion.

Strogatz, S. (2003). SYNC: The emerging science of spontaneous order. *Theia 2003-09-09.* http://www.uboeschenstein.ch/boe/themes/strogatz1.html

Sternin, J. & M. http://www.positivedeviance.org/about_pdi/

Sull, D. & Eisenhardt, K.((2015). *Simple rules: How to thrive in a complex world.* New York: Houghton Mifflin Harcourt.

Vogt, E. E., Brown, J., & Isaacs, D. *The art of powerful questions: Catalyzing insight, innovation, and action.* Mill Valley, CA: Whole Systems Associates Pegasus Communications. https://academy. extensiononline.ucdavis.edu/file.php/1/resources/RM-ArtOfQuestions.pdf

Weick, K. E. (1995). *Sensemaking in organizations.* Thousand Oaks, CA: Sage Publications.

Weick, K., Sutcliffe, K., & Obstfeld, D. (2005). Organizing and the process of sensemaking. *Organization Science*, vol 16, issue 4. http://pubsonline.informs.org/doi/abs/10.1287/ orsc.1050.0133?journalCode=orsc&

Weick, K. E., & Sutcliffe, K. (2007). *Managing the unexpected: Resilient performance in an age of uncertainty (2*nd ed.) San Francisco: Jossey-Bass.

Westley, F., Zimmerman, B., & Patton, M. Q. (2006). *Getting to maybe: How the world is changed.* Toronto: Random House.

Wheatley, M. (2012). *Restoring hope to the future through critical education of leaders.* http://berkana. org/wp-content/uploads/2012/03/RestoringHopetotheFuture.pdf

World Without Genocide website http://worldwithoutgenocide.org/genocides-and-conflicts/ cambodian-genocide

Zimmerman, B., Lindberg, C., & Plsek, P. (2001). *Edgeware: Insights from complexity science for health care leaders (* 2nd ed.). Irving, TX: VHA.

Zinn, H. (2002). *You can't be neutral on a moving train.* Boston, MA: Beacon Press

Appendices

Appendix A - Liberating Structures (LS)

Liberating Structures help groups tackle problems and difficult conversations in new and innovative ways. There is a robust community of practice related to using LS and developing new LS methods. Readers are encouraged to explore www.liberatingstrucures.com and connect with this community. There are more than 35 "Liberating Structures" providing simple designs to ignite conversations.

One Liberating Structure that is familiar, easy, and used frequently in APD is called "1-2-4-ALL," highlighted below. When you have mastered DADs and "1-2-4-ALL", try adding other activities from the classroom that have been successful for including and engaging students to create teamwork and cooperation. Liberating Structures from the website, such as "What I Need from You (WINFY)", "Appreciative Inter- views (AI)", and "Heard, Seen, Respected (HSR)" help generate even more collaboration, learning, and enthusiasm within the team and move the APD process along.

"1-2-4-ALL" (Think, Pair, Share, All)

Sequence: Thinking and talking follows a "1-2-4-ALL" process, which is thinking initially alone, then talking in pairs, then in groups of four, then as a whole.

1. Write down your own ideas – 1 minute.

2. Talk about your ideas in pairs – 2 minutes.

3. Your pair talks about their ideas with another pair (group of 4) – 4 minutes.

4. Each group of 4 shares one most interesting/striking idea with the large group – 5 minutes to share

5. The last step can be repeated if the group has more good ideas to share. Use these guidelines for facilitating 1-2-4-ALL in a meeting:

    *   Space configuration: Set up the space in a way that enables people to move into small groups.

    *   Plunge right in: Get the group engaged and talking about the problem and potential actions quickly. Facilitator introduces about 2 minutes, then facilitates less than 15 minutes of group conversation.

    *   Invite everyone to think about and write down ideas about what we should do about the challenge we're facing.

    *   Shared participation: Make sure everyone has an equal chance to participate. Welcome active contributions. Encourage everyone to speak up. (Remember, you are looking for "unusual suspects" to speak.)

When you are finished, the work in front of the group will be much clearer to everyone – common themes, pressing needs, and a sense of the whole will have emerged. Now, it's time to get into action.

Appendix B: Why do we Keep Asking Questions in APD?

We bring a spirit of inquiry, curiosity, rigor, and fun to asking question in APD. Let's look at why, how, what, and when to ask questions that lead us forward in the process. *Questions are asked and re-asked throughout* the APD process.

What can reiterated and reframed questions do in APD?

- Gather and refine information about our challenge

- Help us to get unstuck

- Help us to learn new ways of working from the bottom up rather than the top down

- Teach one another

- Challenge assumptions about who should be present, who has expertise

- Clarify our own or another person's thinking

- Assist with negotiating

- Encourage creating and innovating

Self-reflection for facilitators, teacher teams, and community members

- Am I seeing the small stuff? What's really happening here? What seems obvious but needs to be called out?

- What is the other person thinking, feeling, wanting?

- What's funny?

- What is my choice right now?

- Who do I choose to be right now?

- What could or should I be asking that would help me understand more?

- What am I assuming is possible or impossible? How do I know?

- What limitations am I assuming about external circumstances?

Am I getting the results I want with the questions I'm asking?

- What other question could I ask?

- What am I responsible for?

- What would *someone else* know about my values from the questions I've been asking?

- How can I change my perspective about what irritates, scares or intimidates me in this conversation?

- Am I asking real questions?

- What am I curious about?

- Is there a question I'm afraid to ask?

Questions to move from being an expert to an active learner

- Am I stuck? Are we stuck?

- Is this working?

- Am I in alignment with values expressed in APD theory?

- How else can I think about this?

- What assumptions am I making based on past experience that may not be true now?

- What's surprising about this situation, conversation, dilemma, person, or me?

- What am I missing?

- What am I avoiding?

- What am I assuming about available resources?

- How can I be more objective, honest, and reasonable?

- Am I seeing the big picture? What's an even bigger picture?

Orienting Questions for the beginning of meetings.

Choose one or more questions for each meeting to support the group members in orienting to and focusing on the work.

- What's on your mind coming into our work together?

- What do we want to make sure happens in our work today?

- What matters most to you about our work so far?

- What is your greatest hope for our work together today?

- What might get in the way of our work today - any distractions, negative predications?

Questions to close a meeting.

Choose one or more questions to bring closure to the meeting.

- What surprised me during our meeting (about the process or about the content?)

- What have I learned?

- What is my next step?

- What is are group's next steps?

Some Wicked Questions

Questions are wicked when no one really already knows the answer. In fact, they don't have easy obvious answers, and their value is that they expose tensions and contradictions and open up new possibilities for thought, evaluation and clarification of values. .
Some examples:

- How can we provide direction without giving directives?

- How can we identify our direction when we don't know the future?

- We've had more success than we expected with our project, but we're not sure which of our efforts contributed most to the success, and people in the group differ in their assessments. How do we decide our next steps?

- How can we be deliberate and intentional about things that emerge without our control or intention?

- If students in a science class come from families who strongly oppose climate science, how can a teacher respect their family values and at the same time convey factual information that is meaningful to them about climate science? Harmon, A. (2017).

- How do people sometimes contribute more by doing less?

- An employee survey in a large organization highlights two strong desires for improvement: people want better direction and feedback from their managers, and they want more autonomy in their work. How can we accomplish both?

- If you discover one of your organization's normally conscientious and effective leaders is doing something you consider unethical, what is your obligation? Do you disclose or keep quiet? Is it ever OK to cover things up for a person with whom you sympathize?

- How can we achieve short term survival goals while working toward a long term vision of the future?

How can you keep your mind in the stars and your feet on the ground?

In the book *Getting to Maybe* (Westley, 2006 pp 168-169) one answer to this wicked question is called the Stockdale Paradox. Vice Admiral James Stockdale was a senior naval officer who survived more than seven years of torture in North Vietnamese prisons. Later he explained how: he maintained unwavering faith that he would survive along with an equally intense awareness of the dire circumstances of his captivity. He says he never confused hope with reality and stayed fiercely focused on both. When a short period of good treatment made him realize he was about to be used in a propaganda film, he brutalized his own face so his image wouldn't be useful. Hope, vigilance, and discipline kept him going. He was released in 1973, received the Medal of Honor in 1976, and finished his naval career serving as president of the Naval War College in Rhode Island. He was later president of The Citadel, The Military College of South Carolina, and a fellow at the Hoover Institute at Stanford University. He also ran for vice president with independent presidential candidate Ross Perot in 1992. He died in 2005.

https://en.wikipedia.org/wiki/James_Stockdale#Early_life_and_education

Appendix C:
How Am I Doing in the Facilitator Role Worksheet

Reflect on each item below. Where are you right now in your work as a Facilitator?

Add any comments that you want to consider for future work. Use this worksheet on a regular basis to reflect on how you are doing in your role.

Commitment to APD process?

Uncertain   High commitment

1   2   3   4

Comments:...
....
....

Comfort with uncertainty?

Difficult   High comfort

1   2   3   4

Comments:...
....
....

Active listening?

Uncertain   Really hearing

1   2   3   4

Comments:...
....
....

Open to surprise and continually curious?

Uncertain   Very open

1   2   3   4

Comments:...
....
....

What could I do better and how could I do that (time, resources, next steps, goals)?

....
....
....
....

Appendix D:
Discovery and Action Dialogue Worksheet

Introduce yourself: Tell the group something about you and why you have come to the group.

- Offer context by talking about the APD approach.

- Share that you are here because your community wants to improve how it is doing on your identified problem. You are interested in finding the solutions and strategies that already exist and great new ideas that are just waiting to be uncovered and used.

Ask the participants to introduce themselves.

- Try to ease into the meeting. Ask participants who they are and what they do.

- Ask whether anyone in the group has had a personal experience with the problem.

Use the following Core APD questions in this order to organize your DAD

- What do you *know* about the problem?

- What do you *do* about the problem?

- What gets in the way of doing what you know you should do and want to do to address the problem? What stops you from doing it every time?

- Do you notice anyone who seems to be successfully overcoming these barriers? Who? What are they doing differently?

- And, very important: Who else should we be asking about this problem or that idea?

- Finally, who wants to volunteer for the next step?

A few reminders

- The Discovery and Action Dialogues may not be linear.

- It is good for the facilitators to have, or ask someone in the group to volunteer, to be a scribe to capture ideas, and read captured ideas back to the group to ensure that they reflect what was meant.

- The "gold" is in questions 4 and 5.

- Your job is to listen. Do not feel like you have to answer or respond to every comment or remind everyone that a "policy exists." Try asking a question and then don't say anything at all until two or three others have spoken.

- Silence is OK. Usually, people are thinking about what to say, and the silence feels longer than it is. Look at the clock and notice that only seconds are passing.

- Try not to judge the value of the comments with statements like "good point" because if you don't say that to everyone, it could make some feel as if their comment is not valued.

- If you comment, try to invite others into the conversation, using phrases like "What do others think?" and "Are we missing anyone?"

- Use active listening and other nonverbal signs to engage quiet individuals. You are welcome to photocopy and distribute this worksheet.

Appendix E:
Buy-in Versus Ownership -
Advice from Henri Lipmanowicz, Plexus Institute

I think it is very, very important to **make a clear distinction between buy-in and ownership** and not present them as if they were the same or interchangeable. It is important because buy-in is what everybody talks about and it more often than not doesn't work precisely because it is the opposite of ownership.

Ownership is when you own or share the ownership of an idea, a decision, an action plan, a choice; it means that you have participated in its development, that it is your choice freely made.

Buy-in is the opposite: someone else or some group of people has done the development, the thinking, the cooking and now they have to convince you to come along and implement their idea without you having been invited at the table upfront before the goose was cooked. They decided without you but now they need your buy-in because without you their great ideas and plans can't get implemented and so are worth nothing. But since you were not part of the process this great idea is a strange one; you cannot fully understand its history or genesis. Since you were not part of the process you cannot be aware of all the other options that were considered and rejected, and of the thinking that went into these choices. You feel ignored, imposed upon, pushed around, unappreciated and your immune system naturally kicks in to reject this foreign idea. You will look like you agree eventually to this new idea because you have no choice and your masters will cheer believing that you have bought in and that you are now as convinced as they are. Your implementation will inevitably be a pale imitation of what it could have been had you been an owner instead of a "buyer-in" and be truly convinced.

What is wrong with buy-in is the notion that it is perfectly OK for a few to make the decisions and then to impose them on all the others and still expect that they will be willing and able to implement them perfectly as if they had made the decisions themselves. **That is a total illusion**. It is an illusion that exists because in most organizations there is no evidence showing the difference between what people can accomplish when they implement ideas they developed together versus what happens when they implement ideas that were imposed on them.

Most organizations have no clue about the value of true enthusiasm and true commitment because they have never seen it. And the reason they have never seen it is because they have never created conditions for people to implement ideas they own without reservations. When experts are working very hard at making plans for others (those they consider non-experts) to execute, it is impossible for them to consider, and least of all admit, that enthusiasm and deep understanding by those others (inferior non-experts) could double or triple the impact of their expert ideas. That obviously would defeat their value as experts!!!

Deep understanding can only be achieved by making oneself the journey of discovery and invention. Someone else's story of the journey will always be a pale imitation of the experience.

If leaders involved UPFRONT all the people that will be involved later on in the implementation there would be **no need for buy-in** for the simple reason that there would be ownership.

Of course the immediate reaction to such a proposition is that it is ludicrous because it is obviously impossible to involve everybody upfront. Wrong!!! Since it is possible to involve all the people afterwards, it has to be possible to involve them all upfront. And therefore the proper question is not whether but how. There are ways and processes from which to choose depending on the circumstances.

Hence my message is: ANYTIME YOU OR SOMEONE AROUND YOU THINKS OR TALKS ABOUT BUY-IN BEWARE! It is a danger signal telling you that your development and implementation process is missing the essential ingredient of involving all who should be. Reconsider your process before you waste a lot of time and energy or achieve mediocre results. One key is to not separate the development of ideas from the implementation of ideas: the same people should be involved in both and it should be one single integrated process.

To conclude, trying to achieve buy-in is most often an attempt to compensate for a problem that should not have been created in the first place, namely the exclusion of all the people whose buy-in is now being sought from the development process. It is a little bit like the need to motivate people; more often than not it is a sign that the real problem is to avoid de-motivating them in the first place.

I have of course oversimplified and exaggerated in order to make my point sharper. Some disagreement and debate around situations when what I wrote doesn't apply should help in making the whole distinction between buy-in and ownership clearer.

Have fun kicking those ideas around.

Appendix F - Self Evaluation Form

This sample sheet from a Maryland multi-hospital initiative helped facilitators assess how small unit-based teams were doing in their APD work. These self-assessments were used to help unit members see similarities and differences in how they thought they were doing (by using the scoring grid at the bottom) and helped facilitators and leaders assess how teams, and different facilities, were progressing in comparison to one another. This form factor is easy to adapt and reproduce. Just remember to keep the ends of each scale consistent with what's shown here.

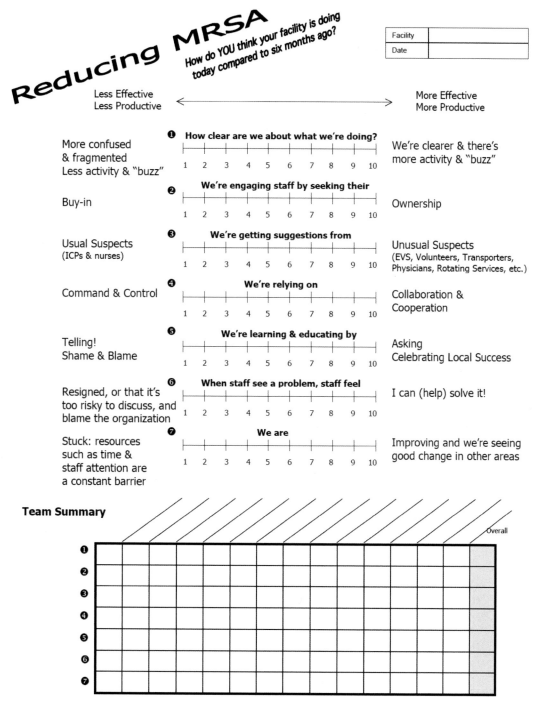

Source: L. Birkes, adapted by S. Benjamin

Resources by Authors Associated with Plexus

Articles

Buscell, P., (2008). More we than me, how the fight against MRSA led to a new way of collaborating at Einstein Medical Center. *Plexus Institute Deeper Learning, Vol. 1 Issue 5,* http://plexusinstitute. org/wp-content/uploads/2017/08/more-we-than-me-mrsa-vol1no5.pdf

Buscell, P. (2008). Pathways to prevention. *Prevention Strategist, Autumn,* 41-45.

Clancy, T. R. (2010). Diamonds in the rough: positive deviance and complexity. *Journal of Nursing Administration, 40*(2), 3-6.

Downham, G., Jones, E., Peterson, P., Mourad, M., Lindberg, C., Patel, P., et al. (2012). Reducing bloodstream infections in an outpatient hemodialysis center - New Jersey, 2008-2011. *Morbility and Mortality Weekly Report, 61*(10), 169-173.

Emerging, (2004) newsletter of Plexus Institute, special issue devoted to Positive Deviance http:// plexusinstitute.org/wpcontent/uploads/2017/08/emerging_2004-august.pdf

Emerging, (2006) newsletter of Plexus Institute, special issue devoted to MRSA and the Plexus Infection Prevention Initiative http://plexusinstitute.org/wp-content/uploads/2017/08/ emerging_2006-december.pdf

Kimball, L., (2013). Changing the organization one conversation at a time. *OD Practitioner, 45*(2).

Kimball, L., (2011). The leadership sweet spot. *AI Practitioner, 13*(1), 36-40.

Kimball, L. (2011). Liberating structures: A new pattern language for engagement. *OD Practitioner, 43*(3), 8–11.

Kimball, L. (2006). Lisa Kimball on liberating structures. Looking forward; tiny conversations with world-class thought leaders & practitioners. http://visionaryleadership.com/

Kimball, L. (2008). Practicing OD in complex systems. *OD Practitioner,* 40(4), 52–54.

Lindberg C, Clancy T. (2010). Positive deviance: An elegant solution to a complex problem. *Journal of Nursing Administration, 40* (4), 150-153.

Lindberg C., & Schneider M. (2012, August). *Leadership in a complex adaptive system: Insights from Positive Deviance.* Paper presented at the meeting of Academy of Management Organization Development and Change Division, Boston. http://c.ymcdn.com/sites/www.plexusinstitute.org/ resource/resmgr/files/li ndberg_and_schneider_-_lea.pdf

Lindberg, C., & Schneider, M. (2013). Combatting infections at Maine Medical Center: insights into complexity-Informed leadership from positive deviance. *Leadership, 9*(2), 229-53.

Lindberg, C., Downham, G., Buscell, P., Jones, E., Peterson, P., & Krebs, V. (2013). Embracing collaboration: a novel strategy for reducing blood stream infections in outpatient dialysis centers. *American Journal of Infection Control, 41*(6), 513-9.

Lindberg, C., Norstrand, P., Munger, M., DeMarsico, C., & Buscell, P. (2009). Letting go, gaining control: positive deviance and MRSA prevention. *Clinical Leader, 2*(2), 60-67.

Lloyd J, Buscell P., & Lindberg C. (2008). Staff-driven cultural transformation diminishes MRSA. *Prevention Strategist* (Spring), 10-15.

Singhal, A., Buscell, P., & Lindberg, C. (2010). *Inviting everyone: Healing healthcare through positive deviance.* Bordentown, NJ: PlexusPress.

Singhal, A., Buscell, P., & Lindberg, C. (2014). *Inspiring change and saving lives: The positive deviance way.* Bordentown, NJ: PlexusPress.

Singhal A., McCandless, K., Buscell, P., & Lindberg C. (2009). Spanning silos and   purring conversations: Positive Deviance for reducing infection levels in hospitals. *Performance, 2*, (3), 78-83.

Zimmerman B., Reason P., Rykert L., Gitterman L., & Christian, J., & Gardam M. (2013). Frontline ownership: Generating a cure mindset for patient safety. *HealthcarePapers, 13*(1), 6-23.

Books

Benjamin, S., Cohn, J., Gardner, L., & McHenry, I., (2016). *Adaptive Positive Deviance Getting Started: How to make big improvements through small (and maybe a few large) changes.* Washington, DC: Plexus Institute Press.

Easton, D., & Solow, L., (2016). *Complexity works!: Influencing pattern-based change in teams and organizations.* http://www.complexityspace.com/

Holley, J., (2012). *The Network weaver handbook, a guide to transformational networks.* Network Weaver Publishing.

Lindberg, C., Nash, S., & Lindberg, C., (2008). *On the edge: Nursing in the age of complexity.* Bordentown NJ: Plexus Press.

Lipmanowicz, H., & McCandless, K., (2014). *The surprising power of liberating structures: Simple rules to unleash a culture of innovation.* Seattle: Liberating Structure Press.

Plexus Institute, (2015). *The Positive Deviance playbook: Developed as collateral for the supporting Teacher Effectiveness Project.* Washington, DC: Plexus Press.

Singhal, A., Buscell, P., & Lindberg, C. (2010) *Inviting everyone: Healing healthcare through Positive Deviance.* Bordentown, NJ: Plexus Press.

Singhal, A., Buscell, P., & Lindberg, C, (2014) *Inspiring change and saving lives: The Positive Deviance way,* Bordentown, NJ: Plexus Press.

Made in the USA
Middletown, DE
23 April 2020